WAKE UP!
IT'S FEEDING TIME

A Professional Athlete's Advice on How to
Succeed in the Game of Life

THE BIG GUY - RYBACK REEVES

Publishing services provided by:

ISBN-10: 1-942761-83-X
ISBN-13: 978-1-942761-83-9

DEDICATION

This book is dedicated to every author who has allowed their knowledge to be spread amongst the universe. With special thanks to Rhonda Byrne and the entire team involved with *The Secret, The Power, The Magic,* and *Hero.* To every moment that I perceived as negative, but in reality allowed me an opportunity to grow and go in a different direction. And last but not least, to the WWE, for as much anger and disappointment as they have caused me, it has allowed me to push harder and drive myself further than I could have ever imagined; thank you.

FOREWORD

It was the end of a very long training day at OVW (Ohio Valley Wrestling) and at that particular time, I was a walk-on athlete trying to secure an opportunity with World Wrestling Entertainment (WWE). Practice was exhausting, and all of the wrestlers were cooling off. One of my fellow wrestlers approached me.

"I feel bad for you, man. Ryan Reeves is coming here next week," said Jack Bull. Jack was a contracted wrestler that had just transferred into OVW from their other farm league, Deep South Wrestling. "What do you mean?" I nervously asked. Jack continued on. "You know the guy from *Million Dollar Tough Enough*? He's about twice the size now, and he's coming here on Monday. He's about 300 pounds of muscle and he's rough. Good luck, Pat."

At that time, I trained alongside contracted WWE developmental wrestlers. OVW was the developmental system, kind of like what minor league baseball is to MLB. These men and women already had jobs and were awaiting their call-up to the main roster. Not me. I was the proverbial new kid on the block, the low totem pole grappler, a bump and feed man, and an unpaid expendable.

Every now and then, a new athlete would arrive into the system. If they had prior wrestling experience or a notable independent wrestling buzz, they could immediately work with more experienced OVW wrestlers on the television show. If they were relatively new, they were put with me to gain experience. I was told I'd be working with Ryan for a few months. It wasn't that I was that good, but I could take the bumps. I could get my butt kicked well, and if I got hurt, well, who cares? I didn't care. I was used to it. I was already conditioned to work matches with giants, former failed football players, shoot fighters, NCAA heavyweight wrestlers and the like. I just wanted a job.

But I had little respect for these outsiders that were just hired for their past accomplishments or their look. I actually hated them. I called them Tin Men because they had no heart and no love for professional wrestling. The true wrestlers (and wrestling fans) felt the same. Ryan was not that. Ryan was the exception to the rule, but I truly believe there was a prejudice against him for the way he was built. People couldn't understand that someone with his prowess was actually a fan of the business. I believe that prejudice followed him his entire career, and fans that don't know him still have that judgment. We had a bunch of matches in developmental, became very close, and through the last ten years have remained brothers (though on different coasts, in different companies, and on completely different paths).

In wrestling, I saw him work tirelessly and then get fired for no reason. After that, I worked 50 hours a week with him for many years at a BBQ joint just so we could afford to live and to keep training and be around wrestling, hoping to get a second chance. He got rehired, when no one thought he would. He gained steam and overcame injuries that should have ended his career. I've seen all the roadblocks and watched him either barrel through or steer around them to continue forward to success. At the time of this writing, he's only 35 years old and it's downright exciting to imagine what his future holds.

This book will let you know who the real Ryback is, both inside and outside the ring. To this day, I don't know of anyone who trained harder, loved wrestling more, or devoted his entire life to it the way he did. He's The Big Guy with the even bigger heart. Enjoy.

Pat Buck

Visit Feedmemore.com and sign-up to receive action-packed motivational messages every week and I'll include exclusive email-only discounts on select Feedmemore.com items. You can shop for great merchandise on the site and order quality Feed Me More natural supplements.

Feed me more, you say? No problem! Join me every week on my podcast, *Conversation with The Big Guy*, along with co-host Pat Buck. The podcast is available on iTunes and Stitcher. Until next time my friends, stay hungry!

CONTENTS

INTRODUCTION

Hello, and thank you for picking up *Wake Up, It's Feeding Time*. My name is Ryback Reeves and you may know me from my on-screen personality, The Big Guy or "Ryback." This book is an accumulation of many things I have learned in my time in this universe and is meant to inform you and motivate you to wake up every day with the goal of being the absolute best version of yourself possible. It is meant to help educate you on a wide array of topics, but to also encourage you to not be afraid to live life now and to take advantage of each day. I spend much of my time in airplanes, hotels, and on the road everywhere from Jonesboro, Arkansas, to the crazy, overpopulated streets of New York City. If you name a country, odds are I have been there. When a guy who has a hunger for knowledge travels the world, it leads to a book like this. The great Napoleon Hill said, "The way of success is the way of continuous pursuit of knowledge," and I truly abide by that each day of my life. All I ask is for you to keep an open mind and if you can get some stuff out of this and apply it to your life, that is great. If you question some stuff, that is great also. I firmly believe that there is no right or wrong in this world, only what we believe. I strive for a world that is filled with love, happiness, and peace, but I also believe in not letting people walk all over you and standing up for yourself if someone else is criticizing you unfairly or attempting to harm you. Life is an amazing thing and we should all understand and respect that.

I will do my best to help you see into my mind. I feel I have always remained humble and stayed true to myself no matter what fame I achieved with professional wrestling. I have always loved wrestling, but I also have loved other things. At this point in my life, I'm known mostly as a wrestler, but I am changing that because I am so much more. I have goals that surpass suplexes and body slams. I want my message of positivity to have worldwide reach, and I want to be the master and ruler of my world. I am an intensely creative being, and I have let my surroundings suppress that for too long. I want to give as much as humanly possible to help others in unfortunate situations. I have enough ideas and goals to last me until the day I die, and now that I am able to devote the time I need, nothing will stand in my way!

I have launched FeedMeMore.com, the home base for my Feed Me More brand, which includes apparel and merchandise along with my Feed Me More nutrition products. I am now an author and already working on my next book, which will focus on my life and wrestling career. There is so much I want to do and experience in life, and I am at that stage of just getting stuff done. I have also launched my own weekly podcast series, *Conversation with The Big Guy*, starring me and my best friend and manager, Pat Buck. It will cover wrestling-related stuff, but it will go much deeper, as we will hold nothing back and speak our truths on anything and everything. I am starting my Feed Me More Fitness Seminars as well, as I have such a passion for nutrition and fitness. I want to show people all over the world that with a positive mindset and ultra work ethic, anything is possible.

I wasn't always this motivated. Before I got into wrestling, I was just a guy who loved working out and playing sports. I had no real direction in my life. As a kid, I excelled in pretty much everything that I did and I had no fears. What I remember most was that I always had fun and loved life. We always hear that we should enjoy being a kid because you are only a kid once, and it's true. Being a kid is so great because the world hasn't yet affected you, and you are experiencing life the way it is meant to be experienced. Well, I am here now at 35 years young to tell you that life is meant to be fun and exciting at all the different stages. It is just up to us to find those things that make us happy! Don't get me wrong—I understand that adults have to work and they have real-life problems. But if we can find that kid in us, life can still be great.

Before I understood about setting goals, I would have glimpses of greatness when I would unknowingly have a goal in my head. There were other times, though, that I was totally lost and just trying to get through the day, oftentimes wanting to sleep my problems away (which never works, by the way). I feel that my bad experiences have helped me to appreciate the good and have also allowed me to feel for others who are in similar situations. It took me losing my dream job, breaking up with a girlfriend I was very attached too, and becoming a full-blown alcoholic for a year before I said enough and took back control of my life. This book is something I am so thankful for because it has allowed me to grow even more as a man. As much as I love wrestling and always will, I have realized there is more to life than fake punches and kicks in a made-up crazy land.

In a way, this book has been therapy for me, and I want it to help you as well. It is never too late to turn our lives around, forgive an enemy, or totally start over. I'm nothing special, just a guy who has always known how to work hard and has always believed in himself even when nobody else did. I want you to know that I believe in you, that you can do whatever you want if you believe in yourself and put forth the action required to accomplish your goals. Trust me, even at rock bottom, the sky is the limit. It is just a matter of taking control of one's life and that only takes one moment. There is a lot of motivational content in our world today. I have had conversations with people who frown upon all of it and are filled with negativity and hate. They think everyone is just trying to get rich and that writing a book is some easy way to rob people and do that. Everything important that I have learned in my adult life has come from motivational or self-improvement books, so I am forever thankful. My mission in writing this is to help some young people, as well as adults, while also reminding myself of lessons learned and continuing my growth as a human being.

I am not perfect, and I make mistakes like everyone else. I try my best to learn and better myself however I can. The world is in a very interesting period and positivity and the desire for self-improvement are at an all-time high, but there is also a lot of bad happening. It is up to us to leave this world a better place than when we came into it, and this book is my way of starting that process for myself. My motto for Feed Me More is simple: "Successful people are always hungry. What are you?" So without further ado, wake up! It's feeding time!

Section 1

HEALTH

TAKING CARE OF OUR BODIES

When we come into this world, we are given one body for the duration of our lifetime. Every decision we make can affect us for good or bad. I feel the need to talk about this subject because of my choice to be a professional wrestler. Being a professional wrestler is probably the last thing the human body was created to do, but somehow many men (and women) have found a way to do it and do it well for a very long time. But it isn't just wrestlers who need to take care of their bodies; it is every single one of us. Our health should be our number one priority, as without it, we can't experience life to its highest level. Despite this, many people don't take proper care of themselves. And while having money or resources at your disposal can make this easier, it isn't necessary. It is our mindset that matters, whether we make it a priority. It is waking up and telling ourselves we are in control and proclaiming what we want from life and not becoming lost souls who let the world control us and dictate our mindsets.

When I speak of being healthy, I mean making smart food choices and drinking water or other healthy drinks such as unsweetened caffeine-free tea instead of sugar-filled or artificial sweetener–based choices. Working out, whether it be yoga, weights, or cardiovascular conditioning, is also important, as is keeping our bodies clean and practicing proper hygiene. Make sure to get into the dentist once or twice a year for regular cleanings and see your personal physician for regular checkups. If your body is stressed from life or work, perhaps you could get weekly massages or see a chiropractor on a regular basis. I get Active Release Therapy once or twice a week, and I wish I had started it ten years ago. If a regular massage therapist is the original T-100 Terminator, then an Active Release Therapist is the liquid metal T-1000! Obviously, we don't all have the same opportunities, but the mindset matters more than anything. One person's goals for a healthy body may differ from another's and that is ok. It all comes back to having balance and a solid understanding of the things around us at all times. Choices we make can affect us for the rest of our lives, so let's do our best to be conscious of this and live our lives to the best of our abilities. It is very easy to take our health for granted and there are so many people who, after having serious health issues, understand what being grateful for good health means because they have experienced it not being ideal. I have had ten surgeries and fully understand what being grateful for our health means. It just takes living one day at a time and making smart choices today so we can feel as good or better tomorrow. We should treat our bodies with the utmost care and respect, and they will return the favor in good health.

NUTRITION

Nutrition is one of the most important things we can learn about, and it doesn't matter at what age we start. Once we understand that what we put inside our bodies directly affects how we act and feel, the results follow very quickly. Obesity is such a problem these days, and while some obesity is caused by medical issues, most of it is caused by bad nutrition and that is something we can control. I became curious about nutrition at a fairly young age. I have always loved food and "feed me more" has literally always been in my vocabulary. When I was a kid and my mother would bake cookies or make Rice Krispies Treats, I would swoop in when she stepped out of the kitchen and eat all the batter or Rice Krispies Treats before she returned. In high school, my mom begged me to cut back on the amount of food I was consuming because the groceries were not lasting the whole week. I would eat bags of chips in one sitting or a box of cereal at once. I was always hungry, but I was very active outside, so I never put on weight. In high school, I started getting informed about protein and would always make sure I had adequate amounts, but I had no idea about carbohydrates and fats. That is why I am never upset when someone doesn't understand that what they consume directly influences how they look and feel. I remember not understanding. I was fortunate to figure it out at a young age. I didn't know nearly as much as I know today about how important every food choice I made was, but I was on the right track.

There is so much information out there and there is no reason why we can't learn and apply it to our lives. When I am learning about something new, I like to read as many different online articles as I can and at least two to three books on the matter to help me understand it. If I knew nothing about nutrition, I would see what the consensus was in online articles and read a few different books on it as well. From there, you start making changes and see what works for you and what doesn't. Having goals about getting a healthy body helps tremendously when trying to form good nutrition habits, as it gives you something to shoot for.

We always hear how balance is the key to so many things and nutrition is no different. Something I learned years ago from one of Tony Robbins books and have applied with great results is that when consuming food, never mix your carbohydrates and your fats. So if you go out to eat and you get naked (non-breaded) chicken wings, a salad, and the salmon, don't add a carbohydrate like potatoes or rice. By doing so, you are combining two energy sources (carbohydrates and fats) and the carbohydrates will increase your insulin production, thus making it easier for your body to store the fat as—guess what?—yep, fat! So consume proteins and fats together or protein and carbohydrates together. Wait two to three hours after eating one to eat the other. I assure you, just applying this method will help you. Everyone's needs will be different depending on your goals, but everyone should keep this in mind when consuming foods.

Something I learned later in life about nutrition that will tremendously improve your health and increase your energy levels is that you should consume more greens, either from eating them or juicing them. Things like broccoli, spinach, parsley, cilantro, cucumbers, celery, and so many others can work wonders for the human body. Be cautious about adding sugar when using a juicer unless it is after physical activity or first thing in the morning when our bodies need a bit of an insulin spike. Stores like Costco sell premade bottles of greens, which maximize your time, and I have been very impressed by them. They are typically found in the vegetable section. My personal favorite is Suja Juice Suja Essentials. Add a glass or two to your day and it will do nothing but good for you. I did have a juicer for about a year, but the motor blew out and I became accustomed to the Suja Essentials.

If there is anything in your life you are unhappy about, you always have a choice to find solutions to your problems and try to feel better about it. If nutrition is something you feel is negatively affecting your life or the lives of your family and friends, take control right now and make the choice to learn more. A lot of the food that is easily available today isn't the right choice. We have to learn what is best for us and our families. Now I'm not saying you can't eat a pizza or have a soda, because that is not ideal for balance. Just understand this world is fueled by business. Our entire system is designed on making money. It is nobody's job to teach us shit. It is our job to learn and control our mind, bodies, and souls. Take control and take the time to figure things out, and I promise you will not regret it.

Look for in ingrediants

ASPARTAME AND SUCRALOSE

Blurry vision

Aspartame and sucralose are two man-made artificial sweeteners used in place of sugar in many low-carb or low-sugar products. Almost all diet sodas and low-carb energy drinks are loaded with aspartame, sucralose, or both. Cough syrups are notorious for using sucralose and, most times, it isn't even listed on the bottle. The key is to be aware and if you experience any of the negative reactions listed below, you may be consuming one of these sweeteners.

Here are some possible side effects of artificial sweeteners found here: authoritynutrition.com/artificial-sweeteners-good-or-bad

- gastrointestinal problems
- migraines
- seizures
- dizziness
- blurred vision
- depression
- blood sugar increases
- weight gain

Here are some other possible negative reactions supplied by Mercola.com.

- Skin – Redness, itching, swelling, blistering, weeping, crusting, rash, eruptions, or hives (itchy bumps or welts). These are the most common allergic symptoms that people have
- Lungs – Wheezing, tightness, cough, or shortness of breath
- Head – Swelling of the face, eyelids, lips, tongue, or throat; headaches and migraines (severe headaches)
- Nose – Stuffy nose, runny nose (clear, thin discharge), sneezing

- Eyes – Red (bloodshot), itchy, swollen, or watery
- Stomach – Bloating, gas, pain, nausea, vomiting, diarrhea, or bloody diarrhea
- Heart – Palpitations or fluttering
- Joints – Joint pains or aches
- Neurological – Anxiety, dizziness, spaced-out sensation, depression

The effects of sucralose (also known as Splenda) on humans have not been studied in depth for long periods of time. Most studies done have been done on animals. Here are the findings of some animal studies involving sucralose (again thanks to Mercola.com).

- Increased male infertility by interfering with sperm production and vitality, as well as brain lesions at higher doses
- Spontaneous abortions in nearly half the rabbit population given sucralose, compared to zero aborted pregnancies in the control group
- A 23 percent death rate in rabbits, compared to a 6 percent death rate in the control group

The following is a list of potential side effects using aspartame thanks to Healthline (www.healthline.com/health/aspartame-side-effects).

- cancer
- seizures
- headaches
- depression
- attention deficit disorder
- dizziness
- weight gain
- birth defects
- lupus
- Alzheimer's disease
- multiple sclerosis

Years ago, I was consuming large quantities of both aspartame and sucralose. I had several health issues that triggered me to look into what I was consuming that could have been causing my problems. I would always get light-headed when getting up out of a chair or when lying down. It progressively got worse over the course of several years in my twenties. I had difficulty waking up in the morning, no matter how much or how well I slept. The most alarming and sudden side effect was that my vision began getting blurry, even though I had always had 20/20 vision. Some days would be worse than others and it was this that caused me to start researching aspartame and sucralose.

I was consuming many diet sodas each day along with other foods and drinks that contained sucralose or aspartame, such as low-carb energy drinks (usually one or two large ones a day), protein bars, protein powders, ready-to-drink protein shakes, and preworkout powders. I can recall being backstage at WWE events and drinking upwards of ten cans of diet cola a day (no wonder I pissed nonstop). I would also use Splenda in almost anything that could use more flavor. As you can see, I was consuming ridiculous amounts of this stuff and not even realizing it. It was literally in everything I was consuming and eventually my body couldn't take it anymore.

I decided to cut it all out cold turkey and it was one of the hardest things I have ever done. I was truly addicted to this substance! The cravings for diet sodas were mind blowing and it was a daily struggle. After a couple weeks, though, I noticed my vision wasn't blurry anymore and waking up was much easier. I had more energy during the day and my light-headedness was no longer an issue. Now, can I say with 100 percent certainty that sucralose and aspartame were the cause of these problems for me? YES, 100 percent, and I have been off of them going on six years now. I firmly believe these chemicals will eventually be taken off the market and stevia will be the sweetener of choice as it comes naturally from a plant. That doesn't mean it is perfect, but it most certainly is better than sucralose and aspartame. I am not saying you have to change everything overnight like I did, and you should always consult a physician before making any sudden dietary changes. But I hope to at least raise your level of awareness about these two substances.

If you are looking for a much safer alternative, look into stevia, which is a natural sweetener. When I designed the formula for my Wake Up! Unlimited Energy Pre Workout powder, I was adamant that we use stevia and other natural flavors. Almost all preworkouts on the market today use aspartame and/or sucralose. I just cannot knowingly associate those chemicals with my brand and ask people to put something into their bodies that I wouldn't put in mine. Hopefully, this will trigger those who do consume these chemicals to do some further research and make the best decision for themselves. Getting off these chemicals is one of the best choices I have ever made.

CAFFEINE! CAFFEINE! CAFFEINE!

I will never forget many years ago when NXT made its debut for WWE and seven other WWE rookies and I were looking to make a name for ourselves. We had to attend a weekly promo class instructed by none other than Vince McMahon (Owner and CEO of WWE). Literally anything could happen in these meetings and being called upon to speak in front of the entire class was a regular thing each week. One day, Vince called upon me and guess what product he gave me to promo? Caffeine! Clearly, my excessive caffeine use was quite obvious. Wade Barrett and I still laugh about that to this day (you may remember him as my co-leader of Nexus).

Most adults consume caffeine on a daily basis—it is in everything from coffee to chewing gum. The coffee and energy drink businesses are making big money because we love this caffeine stuff and we've told them we want more! Up until recently, I was oblivious to how much caffeine was too much. I would sometimes get jittery or have a rapid, irregular heartbeat, but I was shocked to learn that for most healthy people, a dose of 200 to 400 mg of caffeine is considered healthy. Now some people may be able to tolerate a higher intake and some may consume 20 mg and be wired to the gills, but most of us fall into the 200–400 mg range. Recently, I decided my caffeine intake was too high, as I was drinking coffee nonstop along with these diet stevia sodas that also contain 45–50 mg a can. I had no idea how much caffeine I was consuming, but I did know that I had always slept like a baby at night and I was suddenly having some difficulty. After doing some research and finding out how much caffeine was in things like K-Cups, Starbucks Coffee, the diet sodas, and over-the-counter supplements that I thought were caffeine-free but were loaded with it, I was floored to learn there were days I was consuming over 3000 mg of caffeine! Yes, I said 3000 mg. And on the other days, it was easily in the 2000s.

As soon as I found this out, I decided I had to make some major changes. Daniel Bryan had always been an advocate of little to no caffeine and that had always fascinated me. He was superbly conditioned and was always so calm and in control. I figured if Dan could do this, then I could give it a shot also. I limited my intake to under 1000 mg to start. Stopping altogether would have caused a severe crash in energy and that wouldn't have worked for a full-time WWE wrestler. I would have a coffee in the morning and again before my workout and one or two more in the late afternoon. Before long, I was falling asleep more quickly and waking up feeling refreshed, as if I had gotten deeper sleep. So I cut down a little more and a little more over the course of a couple of months. I now have begun doing decaf coffee. (I always assumed decaf meant no caffeine, but in actuality, it does have caffeine, just way less than its regular counterpart. For instance, a K-Cup of Starbucks Coffee contains 150–170 mg of caffeine. At an actual Starbucks, a small coffee contains 180 mg, a medium 260 mg, a large 330 mg, and an extra-large 415 mg. God knows how much you get if you do a red eye or black eye! A McDonald's medium coffee contains 145 mg and a large 180 mg. A large Starbucks decaf contains just 30 mg and a large McDonald's decaf just 18 mg of caffeine.) If you are looking to live a healthier lifestyle and feel you may be addicted to caffeine or consuming too much, consider cutting back. Again, most health professionals say 200–400 mg of caffeine is a safe, healthy amount that provides some great health benefits. Caffeine isn't always listed on food labels (which blows my mind), so it is up to us to be informed and not just rely on others to determine that for us. For my preworkout powder for Feed Me More Nutrition, I made sure to keep the caffeine within the safe range. One full serving has 350 mg of caffeine and 1/2 of a serving is 175 mg of caffeine. I take one full serving before I work out and do decaf coffee the rest of the day. It comes down to being aware of what we are doing throughout the day and keeping track of things like this so that we can correct any imbalances and be healthier overall.

RED RED WINE

Drinking a glass or two of red wine everyday has great health benefits. But you can't drink it with the intention of getting drunk. Too many people hear that red wine is good for us and drink it in abundance. If you do that, you can throw its health benefits out the window. You have to think of this from a health standpoint and drink red wine in moderation. When I first learned of the health benefits of red wine, it was easy to get excited and think that it was a good excuse to get a buzz or get drunk more often. Instead, look at it as you would a freshly juiced drink of greens. You don't drink that to get drunk and if you view your red wine like that too, you will be more than content with your one to two glasses. Also, to make it clear, one glass of red wine is roughly five ounces, so one to two glasses is five to ten ounces.

So, let's talk about some of the benefits of red wine when consumed in a responsible manner. It is great for your heart because the antioxidants in red wine raise your HDL (good cholesterol) and protect against artery damage. A glass of red wine a night has been shown to control your blood sugar. Resveratrol, which is in red wine, has been shown to regulate glucose and insulin sensitivity and to increase our brainpower. It has been shown to slow down the plaque formation in the brain that is often associated with Alzheimer's. People who consume red wine moderately are also less likely to come down with the common cold. A 2010 study in the *American Journal of Epidemiology* found that amongst 4,000 faculty members at five Spanish universities, those who drank more than fourteen weekly glasses of wine for a year were 40% less likely to come down with a common cold. Perhaps one of the most surprising benefits of drinking a glass of red wine could be that it can contribute to weight loss, not something most people would equate with drinking red wine. Research has shown that piceatannol, the chemical compound our bodies convert resveratrol to, has been shown in lab tests to prevent the growth of fat cells. Piceatannol binds to the insulin receptors of fat cells, essentially blocking the pathways necessary for immature fat cells to mature and grow. Now I don't know about you, but this one thing alone is a good enough reason for me to have a glass most nights before bed! Red wine is also great for cooking and can add greatly to many a dish. Having a glass or two of red wine is also a great way to socialize and communicate with family and friends. I don't know about you, but I haven't always been super close to my parents, even though I talk to them daily and love them very much. It is a great way to get everyone together to just talk. Last, but certainly not least, red wine is great at relaxing you and can help those with insomnia sleep more easily. On nights I consume my glass of red wine, I feel nice and relaxed, which allows me to fall asleep almost instantly upon closing my eyes. Hopefully, you can look at this from a health point of view. If you do, you will be singing "Red Red Wine" to all your friends and family.

↙ find out mine

EATING FOR OUR BLOOD TYPE

When I first heard of this years ago, it never really registered with me. At least not enough to research it more. Well, years later, I checked out this book called *Eat Right 4 Your Type* by Dr. Peter J. D'Adamo. Before reading it, I got a blood test and found out my blood type is A positive. Our blood types play a role in our immune system and, according to this book, each blood type processes different food and drinks differently. According to the blood type diet, each type (A, B, AB, and O) has unique characteristics that date back thousands and thousands of years to when the human diet evolved. Knowing what your blood type is and understanding this information could help you if you feel like you are doing things right, but don't feel as great as you think you should. When I stopped eating beef and steak (recommended for Type A), I lost over 15 pounds in 12 weeks, which I would presume was undigested meat inside my body weighing me down. With that said, here is a summary of what I learned from *Eat Right 4 Your Type*.

TYPE O

- Have high stomach acid so type O digests animal proteins and fats better than all the other blood types.
- Typically have unstable thyroid problems

Foods/drinks that are good to consume:

Lean beef, turkey, lamb, chicken, assorted fish, cod, olive oil, flaxseed oil, kale, broccoli, spinach, Ezekiel Bread, blueberries, raspberries, vegetable juices, pineapple juice, black cherry juice, parsley

Foods/drinks to Avoid:

Glutens such as those in wheat breads and grains, lentils, kidney beans, dairy, eggs, cabbage, brussel sprouts, cauliflower, mustard greens, eggplants, potatoes, corn, high acid fruits such as cantaloupe, honeydew, oranges, tangerines, and strawberries, apple juice, black and white pepper, corn syrup, pickled foods, coffee

Supplements for Type O:

Good: Vitamin C, vitamin B, vitamin K, iodine

Bad: Vitamin A, vitamin E, aspirin

TYPE A

- Respond well to vegetarian diets
- Fresh, pure, and organic is great for type As
- Predisposed to heart disease, cancer, and diabetes
- Have low stomach acid and store animal fats easily as fat

Foods/drinks that are good to consume:

Some seafood, lean turkey, lean fishes like salmon, mahi, and tilapia, lean chicken, yogurt, nonfat sour cream, soy, tofu, peanuts, pumpkin seeds, beans, legumes, cereals, grains, wheats in moderate amounts, pastas, broccoli, kale, carrots, spinach, pumpkin, garlic, olive oil, coconut oil, berries, plums, pineapple, grapefruit, lemon, kelp, sugar and chocolate in small amounts, red wine, coffee, green tea

Foods/drinks to avoid:

Fatty meats like beef, steak, ham, hot dogs, cold cuts, lamb, pork, bacon, rabbit, venison, quail, whole milk, cashews, pistachios, kidney beans, lima beans, navy beans, processed and frozen foods, peppers, sweet potatoes, potatoes, yams, cabbage, tomatoes, ketchup, cantaloupe, honeydew, mangos, papaya, oranges, vinegar

Supplements for Type A:

Good: Vitamins B, C, E and iron, Hawthorne, purple coneflower, Echinacea, quercitin, milk thistle, and bromelain (for digestion)

Bad: Vitamin A and beta-carotene

TYPE B

- Can resist a lot more of the serious diseases
- More prone to exotic diseases

Foods/drinks that are good to consume:

Dairy in moderate amounts, lamb, mutton, rabbit, beef, turkey, cod, salmon, flounder, halibut, olive oil, Ezekiel bread, pasta and rice in moderate amounts, potatoes, yams, sweet potatoes, pineapple, ginger, curry, white and brown sugar, green tea, juice

Bad foods/drinks to avoid:

Corn, buckwheat, lentils, sesame seeds, wheat, gluten, chicken, crab, lobster, shrimp, mussels, sesame oil, sunflower oil, corn oils, peanuts, sunflower seeds, sesame seeds, pinto beans, garbanzo beans, rye bread, tomatoes, ketchup, black and white pepper, corn starch, corn syrup

Cinnamon and coffee are neutral for blood type B.

Supplements for Type B:

Good: Magnesium, licorice, bromelain, digestive enzymes, ginseng, gingko biloba, lecithin.

TYPE AB

- This blood type is less than 1000 years old
- Has low stomach acid

Good food/drinks to consume:

Lentils, peanuts, lamb, rabbit, mutton, turkey, yogurt, nonfat sour cream, eggs, olive oil, peanuts, lentil beans, oatmeal, soy, rice flour, fresh vegetables, tomatoes, tofu, grapes, plums, berries, pineapple, grapefruit, lemons, kiwi, sea salt, kelp, miso, garlic

Food/drinks to avoid:

Fatty meats, kidney beans, lima beans, corn, wheat, chicken, smoked and cured meats, flounder, corn muffins, breads, mango, guava, oranges, bananas, pepper, vinegar

Supplements:

*If one adheres to a type-AB diet, there generally isn't a need for extra supplementation. Everyone is different though and this is just a guideline and by no means set in stone, so if you have dietary needs you get from supplementation then definitely stick to it.

SUPPLEMENTS

Over the years, I have tried many different supplements, as I am always trying to maximize my work in the gym and nutrition. I firmly believe that you can't go wrong by investing in yourself and your health. There are a lot of supplements out there and it can be confusing to figure out what we need or what works. The following is a list of the supplements that work for me. I always encourage people to put the time and research in before trying them yourself and making sure your doctor approves before using. Even though I use all of these legal over-the-counter supplements, I am not endorsing or promoting their use in anyone not under direct doctor supervision. This is just to provide you with information that has worked for me over the years. No two people are alike and we all have different nutrition and supplement needs.

Supplements are something I am passionate about. So many of them use harmful sweeteners and other harsh chemicals, so I decided to start my own line of supplements without those ingredients. If you have time, check out Feed Me More Nutrition available at www.feedmemore.com. More and more supplements will be available as it continues to grow. The following are what I currently use in the meantime.

Multivitamin: This should be the foundation for anyone looking to make sure they get all their daily vitamins and minerals. I use AST Multi Pro and take two a day. This is especially important if you are very active and putting in the hard work.

Fish Oil: I use the GNC Triple Strength brand as it is high quality and has no fishy aftertaste or burp effects. Fish oil has a host of benefits and is great for reducing inflammation.

Electrolytes: I started using the Emergen C brand electrolyte a couple years ago, as many of us are deficient in this area. You can drink all the water you want, but if you are lacking your electrolytes, it doesn't always solve the problem. Especially when active and sweating a lot, these can help prevent dehydration on a cellular level and reduce your chances of muscle cramping. I am excited that at Feed Me More Nutrition we are developing an amino acid electrolyte hybrid, which will be very beneficial to athletes and anyone involved in physical activity.

Niacin: I take a time-released niacin, as it is great for blood flow and can help lower bad cholesterol and raise good cholesterol. I especially like to use this before a hard workout.

Creatine: A great addition for any serious weight lifter or athlete. I prefer to use a Kre-Alkalyn type to reduce water retention and bloat. I would not recommend kids use creatine as they have no need for it at an early age.

L-Carnitine: I take this for non-stimulant fat burning and helping with the breakdown of triglycerides (fat) inside the body. There are a host of other benefits, but I primarily use this for three to four months at a time to aid in body fat loss and help with muscle gains.

Green Coffee Bean: Another amazing non-stimulant fat burner that I will use in three – to four-month durations. I go back and forth between this and L-Carnitine to keep my body functioning at optimal levels, as I am always trying to gain lean muscle and decrease body fat. Green coffee bean extract is high in chlorogenic acid and can help burn body fat. I have gotten great results with this supplement and have recommended it to many people who inquire about safe, natural fat loss. There are many different brands of this product, and I like to use one with minimal to no caffeine as some brands have more than others.

Flexcin: This is a joint supplement I discovered ten years ago when I first started wrestling, and I recommend it especially to people who play sports or lift. Even if you don't do that, this supplement would still be worth taking. Flexcin is great for reducing pain from arthritis, lubricating your joints, and decreasing inflammation. It uses all-natural ingredients and is a staple in my supplement cabinet. Healthy joints are as important to strength as muscle, so we need to do our best to protect them.

Super Cissus: A fantastic joint and tendon supplement that I use in conjunction with Flexcin. The added bone and tendon benefits from this proven supplement have worked well for me over the years.

Focus Formula: I started taking this supplement while in WWE developmental. I asked about this brain supplement at the supplement store and the woman informed me that Batista used this one. That was good enough for me. It helps with memory, recall, and concentration, and I find I am just sharper when I take it and able to really zero in on the task at hand.

Vitamin C: With all the traveling I do and the number of people from all over the world I am in contact with, vitamin C is an absolute necessity for keeping my immune system strong. I take two to three thousand mg a day, and if I feel something coming on, will not hesitate to double this amount. My main purpose for using this is for a strong immune system although there are other great health benefits to using vitamin C.

Garlic: I use a brand called Alli Ultra, which uses allicin, an oily liquid found in garlic that has many health benefits. It lowers blood pressure, improves cholesterol, can help strengthen the immune system, has powerful antioxidants that can help prevent Alzheimer's and dementia, and has been shown to help improve blood flow. I absolutely love this all-natural supplement.

Iron: I use a time-released iron supplement as blood work has revealed I am just above low normal in red blood cell count, hematocrit, and hemoglobin. Now most people may be happy with that, but I want higher levels because having a healthy red blood cell count increases the oxygen carrying capacity of the blood, thus helping increase endurance in times of physical activity. Through supplementing, I have improved my red blood cell count, hematocrit, and hemoglobin to a better mid normal range. I prefer to use one called Hema-Plex. Many women are iron deficient and it is something that needs to be addressed if discovered through blood work.

BCAAs: Branched Chain Amino Acids are something I just recently started using. They include the essential amino acids valine, leucine, and isoleucine. They can help aid in muscle recovery and exercise performance. This is one of those supplements that I don't believe will make or break you, but every little nudge in the right direction can add up over time. I use the Sheer Strength brand and am happy with it thus far.

Eye Supplement: I use a GNC brand eye formula to help maintain healthy vision. We are only born with one set of eyes, and I prefer to keep my vision as strong as possible so I don't need the aid of contacts or glasses.

Ribose: This is a supplement I use only before I wrestle as it can help aid in ATP (adenosine triphosphate) and energy production and I'm always exerting a tremendous amount of energy when in the ring. Not only that, but research is showing ribose has amazing health benefits to the heart.

Beta-Alanine: This is another pre-wrestling supplement I use, as it has been proven in research time and time again to increase the amount of work you can do at a high intensity. It is a very cool supplement, but beware that when you take it for the first time, it can produce a tingle effect that can be quite shocking if you haven't experienced it before.

FAST FOOD, OH HELL NO!

On nearly every corner, it seems, lies some sort of fast-food restaurant. Food that tastes so good yet is so bad for us in so many ways. Before I go on, I just want to say I have no problem with these businesses and making money. They are providing a service to neighborhoods everywhere and many have made positive changes to their menus, adding healthier alternatives. It is up to us, though, to have a basic understanding of nutrition and what we put inside our bodies on a regular basis. Consuming this sort of food from time to time is one thing, but for many people, the bulk of their diet comes from the fast-food industry. Even when choosing healthier alternatives, the quality of these items is nowhere near the quality of similar items sold in sit-down restaurants or grocery stores. We all live in this fast-paced world and people with families and many obligations day to day can find it quite convenient to eat at these places to help save time. On top of that, usually the worse the food is for us, the cheaper it is! I feel like a good portion of people assume that just because a place exists and it is so easily accessible that it must be ok to consume on a regular basis. That isn't always the case though, and it is up to us as adults to educate ourselves so that we can pass down the correct knowledge to our children. I will never criticize someone for trying to save money and make sure their kids eat, but people need to be aware that there are healthier, less-expensive options out there if you really look. When we have people who are 400–500 pounds who are getting the majority of their food from these places, we have to take a look at how we are doing things. I will speak below about meal prepping, which is something anyone can do for themselves and for their family. Bulk cooking food for the week for your loved ones truly could save you money and be a whole hell of a lot healthier. Sure, it takes a little effort, but ultimately it is for the right reasons. You could still have your fast-food moments, but just at less frequent intervals.

It is also worth noting not all fast-food restaurants are created equal! There are some great chains out there now that cook their food fresh, use higher quality meats and chickens, and have larger healthy menus. Places such as El Pollo Loco, Chipotle, and Baja Fresh are just a few examples of chains that aren't your typical fast-food restaurant. When I am on the road traveling, I always like to either order room service or go and eat at a sit-down restaurant to start my day. I do the same at night for my last meal, typically, as I find the quality and the way I feel to just be better when I take the time to eat correctly. But being on the road with tight time schedules can create some challenges for finding the right kind of food all the time. Grilled chicken salads luckily can be found almost anywhere these days along with light dressings, and these have been a lifesaver for helping me stay in peak shape year round. There have been times when I have walked into sub shops and gotten a grilled chicken salad and asked for ten extra grilled chicken breasts on the side to have on me for the next four or five hours, so eating better can be done, it just takes a little extra effort.

So why exactly is fast food so bad for us? Because it is usually highly processed food. Processed foods are foods that have been altered from their natural state. They usually have extra fats, sugars, and salts along with other chemicals for preservation and taste. I understand that with the world we live in and everyone having unique circumstances, totally avoiding this kind of stuff isn't always easy, but being aware of it and knowing we have options can do wonders. If you ever stop eating fast food for a lengthy amount of time and then go back to it, you may notice that it makes you feel sick and not quite right. That certainly isn't an accident. If fast food is something you are absolutely in love with and just can't live without, perhaps you can scale back some and save it for once a week as a treat or a reward, but no matter what, know that you always have options.

MEAL PREPPING

Eating in today's fast-paced world can be very frustrating. Remembering to eat healthy can be a challenge, especially with all of the bad food choices on nearly every street corner. Inside the bodybuilding and fitness community, there is something called meal prepping that can help. Meal prepping is just cooking all of your food for the next day or the entire week at one time. You can make anything you want. When I used to cook my meals when I was home off the road, I would usually do thinks like chicken and brown rice, turkey and brown rice, tuna and broccoli, whole grain pasta and turkey, or any combination of them. By setting aside some time once a week, I saved myself a lot of time during the rest of the week. You can buy some of the reusable plastic containers and then store your meals for the week. Preparing this way makes it easier to eat regularly and healthy. There is that prepare word again. Funny how preparation can make life's challenges easier!

I recently met a very nice X-ray technician at a doctor's office. He was an avid weight lifter but had recently had some unwanted body fat gain. We got to talking about nutrition, and I asked him what he did for food while at work ten hours a day. He told me that he never brought food to work and just ate at a local fast-food joint minutes away from the office. I asked him if he was aware that his choice of food was 100 percent the reason for his weight gain and he said yes. When I asked him what he was going to do to change his eating habits he said, "I don't know what to do." I really feel this is how most people who have this problem feel, and it is ok, I totally understand it. I asked him if he had ever considered meal prepping, and I could tell by his demeanor that he was overworked and, with going to the gym most days, he had very little free time. Cooking was out of the question for this guy. So what could he do?

About a year and a half ago, I stumbled upon a meal prep service. Up until this time, I didn't know that existed. The meal prep service industry is booming right now, though, and there are quite a few reputable companies out there. These meal prep services cook and package healthy meals with all the nutrition information listed, so you know exactly what you are getting every meal. I use a company called Fuel Meals that I was referred to by famous pro wrestler Zack Ryder (Thanks, Broski!) I was amazed at how good the food was and, more important, how much time it saved me! I place an order with them and they ship it overnight on ice and it arrives frozen at my doorstep. All I have to do is carry the box inside and then put the meals in my freezer or refrigerator. I eat at least six of these Fuel Meals a day and sometimes as many as eight. Since coming off the road, I am working morning to night and stopping to cook or to run out and get food is quite time consuming when you eat as often as I do. Instead, I just heat one of these meal-prep dishes up in five or six minutes, and I'm done eating within ten minutes. They have changed my life so much by making it easier to consume healthy food when living a hectic fast-paced lifestyle. For people who leave their house for work, all you have to do is put these meals in a cooler with an ice pack and microwave at work, and you can eat clean and healthy all the time. I mention Fuel Meals because that is the company I am sponsored by and I know how good they are. I have a discount code and, if you are interested, I post them weekly on Instagram and Twitter.

Whether you decide to cook your meals or order a meal prep service, either way will ultimately save you time moving forward. Fast food is something that should be avoided most of the time as it just isn't quality food for the most part. Even the healthier options don't compare with other food choices that are available. If finding time to eat is a problem for you, I hope this opens up your options and allows you to reap the benefits of more time, a healthier you, and a better body!

CHEAT DAYS/MEALS

Food is great! Food is energy! Some food tastes amazing! Ever since I was a child, I have been able to put away massive amounts of food. Obviously, though, being in shape and taking care of oneself requires eating a diet that is healthy more often than not. But even people committed to eating healthy like a treat now and then. Cue the cheat meal or day, depending on one's goals. For many people in the fitness industry, such as figure competitors and bodybuilders, the cheat meal/day is a staple of their diets, especially in their off seasons when not competing, and they are a great tool for every single person to have in their arsenal. So what do I mean when I say cheat meal/day? For six days of the week, you stick to a clean healthy diet to help you reach your weight loss or muscle building goals. On the seventh day, you have anything you want for one meal or the whole day.

When I was younger and just learning about nutrition, I would sign into my AOL account (yeah, amazing how old that is now) and research diet and nutrition along with workout advice. I was in high school when I started understanding that the foods I put in my body affected how I looked and felt. I was fortunate to understand this at a young age, so I understand when someone older tells me they have no clue about foods and how much impact they truly have. My senior year in high school (Palo Verde), I would stop at the gas station on the way to school and use my lunch money on Tiger's Milk Protein Rich Bars. I would buy six or seven along with a Red Bull thinking that was eating super healthy. Again, I was just learning about nutrition and hadn't really learned how eating sugars, fats, and carbs all in one sitting wasn't ideal. I actually would have been better off eating the school lunch, but all I saw was that I was eating a lot of protein and protein builds muscle. I slowly started figuring out that I had to make adjustments to what I was doing. I started doing more and more protein meal replacement shakes and whey protein shakes (whey protein is just protein and usually has few fats and carbs, whereas meal replacements have a good balance of carbs, low fats, and an array of vitamins and minerals).

The general rule of thumb when on a healthy diet is to try and do the cheat day or meal once a week. Everyone is different and everyone has different metabolisms, but for the purpose of this chapter, I am going on a once-a-week guideline. When I first started doing this with my diet, I went balls to the wall! I love food and if I was going to consume junk food, dammit, I was going to have it all. I would plan my cheat day for a day where I had nothing to do and I would go to the store the night before and buy boxes of Trix and Rice Krispies Treats cereal, a big tub of ice cream, and a box of twelve Drumstick ice cream cones. I would wake up and eat two boxes of cereal with a ton of milk in huge bowls. I would pass out again and when I woke up, I'd go to this Suncoast Buffet down the road with my buddies and eat brunch. We would sit for hours and my friends would just watch me consume food at a rate that shouldn't be possible. I would then go home with a "food baby" (I've heard this reference twice in two days from women I know and so now it goes in my book), and fall asleep again, usually watching a movie. I would wake up and eat ALL the ice cream and the box of drumsticks and sometimes even drive to this local doughnut shop down the road and buy a large Frisbee-sized doughnut before going back into a food coma. How I stayed in shape and made progress blows my mind still. I would usually wake up the next day early and do hours of cardio to burn off the overabundance of calories I had consumed. Looking back, it always makes me laugh because I hadn't developed self-control when it came to cheat meals yet.

As I progressed, I realized I was overdoing it—A LOT! I was negating an entire week's worth of diet and discipline! I cut down my cheat days to a morning and night meal and eventually to just one meal a day. Today I don't even do it every week, and when I do it is usually something like a pizza and a shake or just some ice cream at home and that satisfies me. The key is to find what works for you and your goals. Some people don't care if they have abs. They just want to be healthy and that is the key thing here. I can say from experience though that doing the huge cheat meals all day long was too much for me and caused me more stress than pleasure. Educate yourself about nutrition and your body to help you make better choices on your cheat meals. It takes hard work and dedication to achieve great things in this world, but we shouldn't cheat ourselves of the great pleasures we have available in the process. Balance is the key. So may the power be with you and don't be afraid to reward yourself for your hard work here and there!

WORKING OUT

There is nothing in the world like working out, and it is never too late to start. Not everyone who works out needs to be a pro bodybuilder or the world's strongest man. It is about being healthy and pushing ourselves. On the journey to better oneself, a workout program should play a strong part. Much like I talk about with nutrition, there are many different workout theories and ideas out there. The question you have to ask yourself (and ideally write down) is, "What do I want?" Do you just want to look a little better and be healthier? Well then, 30–45 minutes a day might be all you need. Maybe it is just going for a nice long walk and doing some light stretching. Maybe you want to start a weight-training program, but you don't know how. There are many great gyms out there and with a little research, you can find a good personal trainer who can teach you the proper mechanics and fundamentals for safe weight training. You can look at videos on websites like YouTube to get an idea of what it will take to perform certain exercises. Working out has so many benefits, such as stress reduction, weight control, endorphin release (feel good chemicals), increased brain power and memory, improved self-confidence, boost in creativity, and improvement of health conditions and disease. On top of all that, it can teach you how to set and achieve goals!

I have loved working out since I can remember. From a very early age, I was always active, whether I was playing sports, jumping on trampolines, or riding bikes. As I got a little bit older, around ten or eleven, I became obsessed with things like push-ups, crunches, pull-ups, and body weight squats. Seeing my mother working out in the living room while my sister and I were just kids contributed to my fascination with working out. I would sit in my room and workout for hours at a time growing up, just doing hundreds of crunches and sit-ups and pull-ups. I was the kid who would beg his parents for all the latest workout gadgets and fads. You know the Tony Little Perfect Sit-up, Ab Flexor, hand grips, forearm builder machines, and much much more. I had no idea about workout routines or nutrition, I just knew I loved pushing myself to physical exhaustion and then doing it all over again. I still remember spending the night at a friend's house and playing Tecmo Super Bowl tournaments. When I wasn't playing, I was seeing how many times I could squeeze one of those handgrips you could buy at the store. I remember doing hundreds of push-ups late at night in my room as I poured sweat and just loving the feeling of having my chest muscles engorged with blood. I think it is 100 percent safe to say I have always been obsessed with maximizing my body. It makes me feel good and when I feel good, all of life just seems easier.

My training methods have evolved over the years, and I am constantly looking for ways to feel better, look better, and become a better athlete. In high school, I would go to the gym and train for four hours straight every day after I did my homework. I had no idea about nutrition yet or that training every body part every day wasn't ideal. I can still recall my routine from that crazy learning period for me. I would start out my four-hour training session in the ab room the 24 Hour Fitness gym had. I would be in there for over an hour every single day because I didn't have abs, and I was absolutely hell-bent on getting abs! People would get to the gym and see me in there and as they were leaving, I would still be in there. Then I still had a three-hour workout to go! I learned the hard way about overtraining at a young age, but it makes me smile that I have always had this insane work ethic and drive. I have tried many different training programs and came up with many of my own and the one thing I have found is hard work always works. If you physically challenge yourself and set goals for what you are trying to achieve, any program can work. It is just a matter of doing what is best for you. So with that in mind, the following is my current training protocol.

At this point in my life and wrestling career, an ideal daily workout consists of three things for me. Warming up and stretching is phase 1. First, I walk for ten minutes or use some form of cardiovascular equipment just to get the blood pumping. Then I begin my active warmup, which consists of body movements starting from the neck and working my way down. Once I feel like my body is in a proper stretching state, I start my stretches. Stretching has helped me tremendously in my wrestling career and has helped me to become more limber. From there I move on to phase 2, weight training, and end with phase 3, conditioning. I use proper nutrition and stretching to stay healthy for wrestling, weight training to keep my body strong for wrestling, and conditioning to keep my endurance for wrestling. These are my goals every day and my approach when working out.

The following is the three-phase weight-training cycle I am currently using and getting great results from.

- 6–8 wks 3–5 reps a set (Maximal Overload Phase)
- 6–8 wks 10–12 reps a set (Mid Maximal Overload Phase)
- 6–8 wks 15–20 reps a set (Low Maximal Overload Phase)

This approach allows me the best of all worlds. I am hitting fast twitch muscle fibers and slow twitch muscle fibers and, while in my Low Maximal Overload Phase, I am concentrating on ideal form and giving my body a chance to rest from the burdens heavy training can have on your body if done constantly. When you are constantly breaking down your body by wrestling, you have to find time to let your body normalize. This approach builds muscle and constantly allows you to make gains. Each phase, I progressively move up in weights and I am finding I just keep improving. I also want to stress how important focus is when weight training. I squeeze the muscle as hard as I can at different positions of the movement and envision the muscle growing and developing how I want it with each rep. When I was younger, I would just throw weights around and while that will get results, it doesn't even compare to when you really zone in.

Conditioning is something I have become obsessed with over the years. I truly believe that the work you put in to this one particular area can reap you the greatest rewards over time, especially for athletes, fighters, and wrestlers. If you can outlast your opponents, recover more quickly in moments of intense force, and still have energy at the end of a game/match/fight, you increase your chances of success! I try to constantly challenge myself in this area with things like burpees, jump rope, slam ball throws, tire hammer strikes, jumping jacks, mountain climbers, assault bike, box jumps, using the elliptical machine while wearing an elevation training mask, and the list goes on and on. I have had to always do a lot of conditioning because I'm so big. The more muscle you have, the more oxygen your body consumes. I get so upset with myself if by chance I feel tired, because I work too hard to show that weakness. But I am human and it happens at times. I do my best, though, to minimize those times.

Below you will find a breakdown of my training program for each body part.

CHEST

- Incline Barbell Press 4 Sets
- Flat Dumbbell Press 4 Sets
- Hammer Strength Incline Press or Incline Machine Press 4 Sets
- Pec Deck Flies 4 Sets
- Bosu Ball Push-Ups or Perfect Push-Ups 3 Sets

BACK

- Pull-Ups (weighted when training 3–5 reps and normal when doing 10–12 rep range) 4–5 Sets
- Lat Pull Downs (only when I'm in 25–30 rep range) 4 Sets
- Barbell Rows (3–5 rep range and 10–12 rep range) 3–4 Sets
- Machine Row or T Bar Row (25–30 rep range) 3–4 Sets
- Deadlifts 3–4 Sets
- Close Grip Pulldowns 3 Sets
- Straight Arm Lat Pull Downs 2 Sets
- Pulley Rope High Trap Pulls 2 Sets

LEGS

- Barbell Squats 4–5 Sets
- Front Barbell Squats 2–3 Sets
- Leg Extensions 5–6 Sets
- Glute Ham Raises 5–6 Sets
- Single Leg Pistol Squats (no rep range on these; I just try to do as many as I can) 2–3 Sets
- Inner Groin Thigh Machine 3–4 Sets
- Glute Kick Backs 3–4 Sets

ARMS

- Preacher Curls 3–4 Sets
- Barbell Curls 3 Sets
- Hammer Strength Curls 2 Sets
- Dumbbell Concentration Curls 3–4 Sets
- Overhand Grip Barbell Curls 1–2 Sets
- Ring Dips or Parallel Bar Dips (weighted for 3–5 rep range and 10–12 rep range and body weight for 25–30 rep range) 4–5 Sets
- Flat Back Dumbbell Tricep Extensions 3–4 Sets
- Rope Tricep Pushdowns 3–4 Sets
- Straight Bar Reverse Grip Tricep Extensions 2–3 Sets
- Dumbbell Tricep Kickbacks 1–2 Sets

SHOULDERS

- Seated Dumbbell Shoulder Press 3–4 Sets
- Hammer Strength Shoulder Press 3–4 Sets
- Side Lateral Shoulder Raises (thumbs up grip) 4 Sets
- Machine Rear Delts 5–6 Sets
- Straight Bar Upright Rows Wide Grip 2–3 Sets
- Front Dumbbell Raises (thumbs up grip) 2 Sets
- Overhead Squats (a superior exercise for all around core and shoulder stability) 4–5 Sets

TRAPS (DONE TWICE PER WEEK AND WILL PICK ONE OF THESE EXERCISES) 4-6 SETS

- Barbell Shrugs
- Hammer Strength Shrugs
- Dumbbell Shrugs

CALVES (DONE TWICE PER WEEK) 6-8 SETS

- Seated Calf Raises
- Straight Leg Seated Calf Extensions

NECK

- 4 Way Neck Machine 8–10 Sets (all directions = one set)

FOREARMS (DONE ONCE OR TWICE A WEEK)

- Captains of Crush Hand Grips 8–10 Sets

RESTING THE BODY

Anyone who works out on a regular basis and enjoys pushing themselves will understand how important it is to rest the body. For those who work out but maybe don't enjoy the process quite so much, you will probably rejoice and scream with joy over what I am about to talk about. It is imperative we give our bodies a break from time to time from physical stressors such as weight training or other activities that stress our muscles, joints, and tendons. I first started learning about proper weight training as a kid from a natural bodybuilder named Jeff Willet, who looked larger than life and did it through hard work and diet. Jeff always advised taking a week off after every nine to twelve weeks of intense weight training. I did this early on in my weight-training journey, but somewhere along the way, once I began wrestling, that all changed. I don't know if it was the wrestler mindset of go go go that eventually takes over anyone who reaches the professional level or if it was just me being so hard on myself that I couldn't ease up every once in a while. Since I started wrestling, the only time I have ever taken off from the gym and intense conditioning is when I have been injured. Being 35 years old at the time of this writing, I realize I have made a major mistake and paid the price for not giving myself proper rest periods. I sit here now, three and a half weeks since I've touched a weight and one more week to go, and I am finally at peace with it. I chose to have an old ear perforation and broken nose/deviated septum injury fixed to get my health in order as I take a little break from the whacky world of pro wrestling. It required no weights for four to five weeks to let everything heal. In that time, my back, which has been getting muscle spasms and muscle weakness when I wake up from sleeping, and my right shoulder, which was beyond tight and screaming at me to just chill out, have both totally calmed down and feel better than they have in a long time.

Wrestling four to five nights a week for the past five years and nonstop heavy weight training along with high-intensity conditioning with things like burpees was breaking my body down over and over, and I wasn't giving it any time to relax and rest. Ideally, what I should have been doing is taking seven to ten days off of weights, if not a full two weeks, every three to four months to let everything calm down. I am so hard on myself, though, and feel like if I am not in the weight room or doing something to benefit myself, I am moving backwards. That is so totally ridiculous looking back at it all. I always feared I was going to lose too much muscle. God forbid I drop a few pounds and let my body heal. And besides that, it never is that bad. I have learned that if you keep your nutrition point on, you hardly notice a difference! Letting our bodies rest will allow us to refresh ourselves and come back even hungrier. My last week in the gym I was struggling because I was so beat up. I had plateaued in several different lifts because of nagging injuries. Anyone who is serious about fitness understands this mindset. I love lifting weights and getting that pump and pushing myself time and time again, and I want to be able to do that all the way until the day I move on in the universe. But we have to be smart enough to look at the big picture.

Besides the physical break we get from taking seven to ten days off, it also gives us a nice mental break. There are only 24 hours in a day to get things done and this gives some of those back. If you suddenly have a couple extra free hours in your day, you can do some things you always put off because you're so busy. Getting ready to work out, making your shake, driving to the gym, working out, driving home, and then having another shake or making food takes up a good chunk of time. With that time back, you now have options, so use your imagination and make the most of it! Life is so much more enjoyable pain-free, trust me when I tell you that. So let's stay hungry, bust our asses when we train, and be smart enough to give ourselves seven to ten days off every three to four months or when we just know something isn't quite right.

WAKE UP

For a large part of our population, waking up is a dreadful and ago-nizing experience. For another portion, though, it is a wonderful experience that leads to another amazing day of life here on this planet. I am a firm believer that the thoughts we have in our heads when we go to sleep at night determine how we wake up in the morning. If we go to sleep in fear, just trying not to think about life or our problems, then I believe we will wake up dreading the day. And we'll still have to eventually deal with our problems. We have to make a conscious decision when we lay our heads down at night to turn our thoughts to positive affirmations, which will improve our lives and help us be thankful for what we already have. For a lot of people, nighttime is when their brains start going in all different directions and the negative thoughts creep in. It isn't supposed to be this way, though, and recognizing those negative thoughts is imperative to having more positive thoughts. I am a firm believer, though, that our mental state before bed plays a huge role in our quality of sleep and how we wake up.

There are a lot of different theories about much sleep we need each night. The old adage used to be that eight hours was the magic number. Recent studies claim seven hours is the new eight. I have heard stories of some of the most successful people in the world functioning on four to six hours of sleep, and some people claim they only sleep two hours a night. My personal opinion is that we are each different and have different needs, but how we go to sleep at night plays a huge part. If we go to bed knowing we will get a solid eight hours, we feel confident that we are going to feel good. If we know we are going to get three hours of sleep, we assume we are going to feel horrible and be exhausted the next day. We feel these thoughts because of what we were taught or what we presume to be true about sleep. I feel that if we use positive affirmations and truly believe them, we will wake up feeling refreshed and alive no matter how much sleep we get. When I lay down, I pick the number of hours I'm going to get that particular night and say, "Tonight I am going to get an amazing seven hours of deep restful sleep and wake up feeling refreshed and energized with unlimited energy for the entire day. Thank you for this deep sleep." I do this no matter what the amount is, as it varies from night to night due to my professional wrestling job and the running of my Feed Me More business.

While there are times when I have no choice but to get five to six hours, I prefer seven whenever I can. I feel for elite athletes and people who push their bodies because getting adequate amounts of rest to let the body repair is extremely important. If you are anything like me and going hard from morning to night, you will understand where I am coming from. If you find that sleeping four hours a night satisfies you and you are firing on all cylinders, then that is great. If you need more, that is ok too. There truly is no right or wrong and it all depends on the lives we are living and our goals. Life is more fast-paced and chaotic than ever before, so trying to improve ourselves in the area of sleep would do us all a lot of good.

Another habit that could help you wake up in the morning is to place your alarm clock away from the bedside. If you use your cell phone as an alarm, placing it out of arm's reach at night is a must. For those who need their phones within reach for emergencies, make sure you place an alarm clock a good distance away. The reason for this is very simple. How many of you hit the snooze button time and time again every single morning because you don't want to get up? I am sure most of us have done this more than once! By placing your alarm away from your bed, you force yourself to get out of bed to shut it off. Doing this greatly enhances your chances of staying awake. If you want to increase your chances even more, then immediately get in a cool or cold shower. You will feel your nerves awake throughout your entire body immediately! I love to do this and then slowly work it back to a hot shower once I'm awake to help loosen up my muscles, which often can be quite stiff upon wakening.

Obviously, there are many different things that can affect sleep, but taking a positive approach to it can help. As far as our cell phones go, it is smart to turn off notifications so you don't get woken up by the beeps at night. Also, don't hang out on the phone in bed as the light from the phone can make it harder to shut down. Making sure there are no lights anywhere in the room is ideal and many of us sleep best in a cool room. I like a high-powered ceiling fan along with the air at 72–73 degrees. Everyone is different, but if you are struggling, these are some things to try.

You may be wondering about the use of sleep aids. I have tried many different sleep aids over the years, such as NyQuil, Dream Water, Zzzquil, melatonin, and a host of others. I feel we are better off not using these and find I get my best sleep using no drugs and just making sure I haven't had caffeine too close to bed. Also, a lot of melatonin products have way more melatonin than we need and when taken in excess, it isn't ideal for our bodies. There are six all-natural options available to us that I keep on me at all times just in case I need to sleep on a flight or get to sleep ASAP: GABA, passionflower, chamomile, lemon balm, valerian root, and ZMA (zinc magnesium aspartate). When taken together, they can provide you with a calm relaxed feeling to help you fall asleep. I have also noticed no hangover symptoms with this combination. I'm actually in the process of having my very own sleep supplement formulated for Feed Me More Nutrition so you could take one supplement rather than six different pills. This is easier, not to mention cheaper. In the meantime, you could order these on Amazon or elsewhere online and see for yourself how well they work together. As always, consult your physician before taking any over-the-counter supplements.

Sleep is an important part of every single one of our lives, so let's master it and wake up with the intentions of being the best versions of ourselves each and every day and night!

SLEEP APNEA

The Mayo Clinic defines sleep apnea as "a potentially serious sleep disorder in which breathing repeatedly stops and starts. You may have sleep apnea if you snore loudly and you feel tired even after a full night's sleep." According to Dr. Foldvary-Schaefer, Director of Cleveland Clinic's Sleep Disorders Center, 9 percent of women and 24 percent of men have sleep apnea. About 80 percent of people with it are undiagnosed. I was one of them until several years ago. I take pride in being as healthy as I can, but this is one thing I was totally clueless about. I want to increase awareness because, if left untreated, it can take years off of your life. I remember seeing a video of me when I was around five years old and I was snoring extremely loudly. I firmly believe I have had sleep apnea my entire life, but I had assumed my snoring problem was from a deviated septum from a broken nose early on in my wrestling career. I started to get concerned when I was around thirty years old and I started nodding off behind the wheel when driving between cities after a wrestling match. Also, when sitting down to watch TV or something I would almost always fall asleep. I could never understand why I couldn't focus and watch an entire show.

The following are some other symptoms of sleep apnea.

- Sleep: excessive daytime sleepiness, insomnia, nightmares, sleep deprivation, or snoring
- Respiratory: episodes of no breathing, breathing through the mouth, or loud breathing
- Also common: depression, dry mouth, dry throat, fatigue, headache, irritability, mood swings, or weight gain

I finally set up an appointment at Zeeba Sleep Centers in Las Vegas. They monitored my sleep over five hours one night and discovered that I was right; I had sleep apnea.

I was set up with a CPAP machine (Continuous Positive Airway Pressure) and have grown accustomed to it. Apparently having a large neck wasn't helping my cause either. Ever since I was a kid, I have been fascinated with having a large, strong neck, as I always heard that the best boxers had a strong neck and that the bigger and stronger it is, the better able you are to take a punch. Well, that was good enough for me, so I have used a neck machine once a week for as long as I can remember. Even now in my own gym, I have my very own neck machine. Problem is, the bigger your neck is, the greater the chance your air pathway will be constricted when you are sleeping. Your neck muscles relax when asleep and expand, narrowing your air passageway and increasing your chances for snoring and sleep apnea. My neck is 21 inches and the doctor said anything over 18 almost ensures you will have sleep apnea to some degree. There is actually a surgery that has a great success rate at curing sleep apnea by removing tissue from the throat. Eventually I plan on having this done, but in the meantime, I have actually grown quite accustomed to my CPAP machine.

Since starting my CPAP machine (the mask attaches to my face at night), my life has improved tremendously! At first it wasn't easy as I found it a bit uncomfortable, but I started feeling better even if I only wore it a few hours a night, so I became motivated to try and keep it on as much as I could. Taking the mask off at night is a very common issue, as it can be uncomfortable and even a bit scary if you aren't used to sleeping with a mask on (I mean, really, who would be?). Now I cannot imagine sleeping without my CPAP machine and find it very soothing and comforting. I sleep five or six hours and feel better than ever, and I no longer fall asleep while sitting down or driving. My life has improved tremendously!

There is also a surgery that can be performed that has a very good success rate at curing or greatly improving your sleep apnea. It takes one to two weeks to recover from and, if successful, eliminates the need for a sleep apnea machine. I am looking into having this done next to increase my health further as it is sometimes difficult to wear the sleep mask on planes. And let's just be honest—as much as I love it, it is a medical device and just doesn't feel cool! A good ear, nose, and throat doctor should be able to tell you everything you need to know about this surgery if that is the option you choose.

I cannot stress to you enough how serious sleep apnea is. If you have a friend or a loved one you suspect of suffering from it, please recommend they make an appointment at a sleep study center. And get in yourself if you think you have sleep apnea. Sleep apnea can take years off of your life, so let's raise awareness! Whatever option you choose, I promise you that you will not regret giving your body the oxygen it needs!

BREATHING

Breathing is something that has never come easy for me. I always had difficulty breathing through my nose and after a couple hits to the nose early in my wrestling career, it became nearly impossible. I became a full-time mouth breather. As mentioned early, I have always snored and I have sleep apnea. I recently had nose surgery and can finally breathe normally. It is an amazing feeling being able to breathe properly through your nose!

Years ago, I was introduced to diaphragm breathing by my good friend former WWE World Heavyweight Champion Daniel Bryan. Diaphragm breathing is breathing that is done by contracting the diaphragm, a muscle located horizontally between the thoracic cavity and abdominal cavity. Air enters the lungs and the belly expands during this type of breathing. It doesn't seem overly complicated, but when you cannot breathe through your nose well, it is hard to truly "belly breathe." There is a book called *Breathing* by Andrew Weil that I feel could benefit everyone wanting to learn how to breathe properly. It helped me tremendously and I practice it every day, typically in the morning, in the afternoon, and at night before bed. Belly breathing can help reduce the stress hormones adrenaline and cortisol and is a great stress reliever. It can also lower your blood pressure. Some other great benefits are:

- Helps lower blood sugar (lowering risk for diabetes)
- Releases serotonin (the hormone that makes you feel good)
- Improves your sleep quality by helping you relax
- Increases blood flow to the prefrontal cortex of the brain
- Increases secretion of growth hormone
- Gets rid of free radicals in the body
- Can help with regular bowel movements, eliminating constipation

- Increases energy of the immune system
- Can help improve your skin over time by helping reduce stress

I don't know about you, but all this stuff sounds pretty damn good to me! I recommend you read at least one book on diaphragm breathing, but I will try to explain it as best I can. Start by either sitting or lying on the floor and relaxing. Breathe in through your nose as deep as you can, allowing the air to fill and expand your belly. Give it a beat and then exhale through your mouth, pulling or sucking your diaphragm in until all of the air has been expelled from your body. Do this for three to five minutes, once or twice a day. There are all sorts of different breathing exercises that you can find in books or online, but this is the gist of it. The health benefits make it a no brainer, so add it to the things you do in your day. All I ask is that you commit to it; just don't do it for a few days or a week then stop. Do it as many days as you can and if you miss a day, do it the next day and get back on track. After a while, it becomes second nature. I assure you this is one thing that you will not regret if you do it properly and consistently!

Diaphragm
breathing once/twice a day
(watch video)

SEXUAL ENERGY AND CONTROL

Sex sells! Sex is all around us in television, movies, magazines, billboards, video games, online—you name it and sex is being advertised. We are sexual beings and it is perfectly healthy behavior to want sex. The problem comes when that sexual energy and impulse starts to control your entire existence. Many people become prisoners of this great sexual energy. If not controlled and harnessed, it can become very destructive to one's life and well-being. When we as humans feel a strong sexual urge, the first thing that goes through many of our minds is to release this energy via some form of sexual stimulation, whether alone or with someone else. Sadly, many horrendous acts have happened from men and women not being able to control these sexual urges. While there is nothing wrong with wanting sex or instant release, it can cause real trouble if it takes you over and you become helpless to its powers. Sexual energy is perhaps the strongest energy that exists within us, so I feel it is worth discussing how to channel that energy for other beneficial activities and gain more control over oneself. I'm not saying that if you choose instant relief that is wrong, because it isn't. But if you are reading this and saying, "I know EXACTLY what The Big Guy is talking about," then you get it. Enjoying sex is a privilege and a celebration of our physicality. If we become prisoners to this energy, it can lead to unwise acts, overindulgence, restlessness, violent acts, or outbursts along with numerous other negative things. Easy online access to porn and dating sites or sex sites and apps makes it even harder for us to remain in control of our sexual urges. I am not stating that if you use these things you should cut them out, but we need to be conscious of these things and if we are feeling like a prisoner to our sexual urges, then we need to look at what we are doing. Cutting down or eliminating some of these things may make it easier for us to gain some much-needed control.

Sexual energy is a positive emotion, but sometimes we allow it to be used in a negative manner, and that is what we want to avoid. One of my favorite books, *Think and Grow Rich* by Napoleon Hill, talks about how all the influential people he had ever interviewed had strong sexual urges, but they were able to channel this energy. When you can control this energy, you will see how you can use it to get things done that you maybe had overlooked before or were too tired to attempt. I am not saying you should never act on your sexual urges, but that you should be more aware of them and understand how powerful this energy is within us.

Sex allows us to create new life; it is that powerful. The next time you feel an intense sexual surge of energy, don't immediately try to get rid of it. Just sit in the moment and be completely aware of what you are feeling. Feel the energy throughout your entire body and if it is overwhelming, look at my section on breathing. Do your best to contain this energy and, if you can stick to your guns, you will feel it give you an amazing sense of power. You will feel euphoric and almost invincible once controlled. There truly is no other energy equivalent to that of sexual energy so why not harness its powers for other areas of our life and not just sex. (Don't get me wrong—that is still and will always be our number one favorite use.)

Life is about learning about ourselves and this is a very important matter that can help us all if mastered.

OUR BRAINS AND PORN

As I have grown and evolved in my life, I have had the opportunity to meet many people from different walks of life. I have found porn stars to be some of the most unique and interesting people I have met. The ones I have encountered are very genuine, nice women who just happen to really enjoy sex. They are human beings like each and every one of us and while some of you may not agree with their lifestyle choice, it isn't your right to judge. If they are happy, that is all that matters. The way someone makes a living is an individual choice.

But that doesn't mean that porn isn't problematic. A friend of mine once told me that the majority of guys she met and dated had performance anxiety when she became sexually involved with them. I did some research online and combined that with my personal experience to come to the conclusion that our brains are getting desensitized from years of watching porn. The ready availability of porn and the wide range of types of porn only make this problem worse. When my generation was entering the early years of adulthood, our thoughts or perhaps pictures from a magazine like Cosmopolitan or Victoria's Secret were more than enough to get the job done. But now, with the easy availability of pornography videos, we've moved on from still images to watching these fantasies play out over and over on screen. As time goes on, some men begin to have trouble masturbating without some form of visual stimulation. My friend in the porn industry wholeheartedly agreed that men who watch a lot of porn could find themselves not as stimulated when in the real moment of sex. Their brains become desensitized and real sex becomes less appealing than the videos they have become accustomed to watching.

So what is the solution if this is a problem for you? There is a great website called YourBrainOnPorn.com that discusses strategies and studies and gives the real-life recovery stories of many men. The bottom line is that you need to stop masturbating to porn and instead use your mind to mentally arouse yourself. Over the course of several weeks, your brain will begin to return to normal. I have applied this to my life and it has made the act of real sex a thousand times better and more exciting. I am not saying you have to give up porn for good, but gain control over your consumption if you feel you have a problem. Give yourself a break from time to time. Balance truly is the key to most things in life and when it comes to our brains and porn, it most definitely applies.

OVERCOMING ADDICTION

Everywhere I go, I see people smoking or using chewing tobacco. I will spare you the countless statistics on the dangers of these products and just offer you some insight from someone who has battled nicotine addiction off and on for about ten years now. It started when I was 24 years old and wrestling in the WWE developmental system OVW in Louisville, KY. I was on my way to one of our wrestling shows and had given a ride to one of the guys. We stopped at a gas station and he insisted on buying me something to say thank you for the ride. I had food and drinks so he asked if I wanted a can of dip (smokeless tobacco). I had noticed quite a few of the other wrestlers using this stuff at our shows when there was downtime but had never paid it any mind. I didn't really think anything of it and said yes to be nice. I 100 percent should have known better than to allow that stuff anywhere near me. That one moment ended up playing a major role in my life. We got to the show and I put a pinch in my lower lip. Within seconds, I was flooded with a buzz unlike anything I had experienced. It was incredible! After a couple minutes that buzz turned to absolute disgust as I became very nauseous. I took the tobacco out of my mouth and ran to the bathroom to wash my mouth out. The sickness lasted hours. I never threw up, but had a weak sick feeling that I wanted to go away as soon as possible. I was supposed to have the night off from our wrestling show that night, but after some influential people saw me sick, they thought it would be cute to see me wrestle. I did just fine that night despite being completely nauseous.

Little did I know at the time, but I had just become hooked on chewing tobacco. Some people try it, react the way I reacted, and never touch the stuff again. Then there are people like me. I remembered that buzz it had given me and that was enough to make me try it again later that night. This time, I got the buzz, but didn't get as sick as the first time. The next day I repeated the process, getting a little less sick each time. Before I knew it, I was a full-time user of chewing tobacco, or a dipper, as we call it. I would wake up, eat breakfast, and put a dip in. After a great workout, I would put a dip in. After every meal, for sure, a dip would go in. Before bed and brushing my teeth, a dip would go in, as well as at any other times I felt the need (which was a lot). The strong buzz it once gave me faded over time, but I just truly seemed to enjoy the whole process. In reality, it was just true addiction to a harmful substance and my mind was playing games with me. I would try to convince myself that it made me happy and that it wasn't the nicotine I was addicted to, but rather the wintergreen flavor. It is funny how the human mind will trick you when you want something badly enough. You will lie to yourself that what you are doing is totally acceptable. But personally, I don't think doing something that causes so many side effects and causes cancer is acceptable if you have a family and even remotely love yourself. NO VAPING

With chewing tobacco, mouth and throat cancer is a big risk. I still remember a man by the name of Steve Williams, who was known in wrestling as Dr. Death. The man was as big and as tough as they came and he came down to the OVW school to help out with the training from time to time. His wrestling career was over and he had just battled a bout of throat cancer. I had not seen him in a while and when he came back down, he had a hole in his throat! Even though I saw this up close and personal, I didn't want to stop yet. He caught me putting in a dip one day and proceeded to lecture me on not making the same mistake he had. I took it out and made sure not to do it when he was around, but I was still using it when he wasn't. But his words and what he'd gone through made a lasting impression; it just took time to settle in. Mr. Williams has since passed on, but thank you sir for playing a huge part in me stopping.

I noticed fairly quickly that the tobacco would sometimes make me very tired to the point I wouldn't want to do anything except just relax and enjoy the dip. This didn't always happen, but either way I wasn't nearly as productive of a human being while using it. I would read less and listen to fewer audio books and was more lethargic than normal. I had to drink lots of coffee when I dipped just to feel somewhat normal, which was just adding to my overconsumption of caffeine. I remember wanting to stop fairly early into my use and not being able to. A couple of years later I finally was able to stop cold turkey for a period of about three months. Then something triggered me to do just one pinch and the process started all over again. I quit again several times, sometimes for up to a year and half, but always went back. It is beyond difficult. The first few days are pure hell as it seems as if you have truly lost something you loved so much. That feeling is addiction and our minds will play games with us to try to get us to give in and give our body what it thinks it so desperately needs. I now understand the repercussions a moment of weakness can have on me, so I am content not using it ever again. I have also experienced some minor side effects—such as a major recession in my lower gum line that will eventually need a gum graft repair—and that is enough for me. I don't want to ride it out long enough to see serious side effects.

Another common addiction that I dealt with for over a year is alcohol addiction. It is readily available and so easy to get addicted to. Having a need for it can take over very quickly, if you let it. Over 18 million people are estimated to be addicted to alcohol, and there are many others who engage in risky binge-drinking patterns that are reckless and destructive. My addiction to alcohol started when I was released from my WWE developmental contract at the age of 25. I met a woman whom I was very much in love with and moved into her house to help her raise her two-year-old child. For as many good qualities as she had, she loved to smoke and drink—a lot! As I have said, you are whom you surround yourself with, and I began drinking with her more often than not. She enjoyed drinking at night, and it became something we did together every single night as we would watch TV or a movie before going to bed. It seemed so harmless at the time.

On days I was off or didn't have to work late, I started drinking earlier in the day. I felt lost in life and the alcohol made me feel so good. It would help me forget my problems temporarily, but the next day the problems were still there. When my girlfriend and I broke up, it left me in an even lower place. I moved into a disgusting little studio apartment, and I would work and workout and just drink and drink and drink along with using chewing tobacco. At first I only drank at home at night, drinking until I passed out. Eventually, I started keeping a giant drink in my car when I was working as server, and I'd chug it before going in. I would sneak out to my car during work with a diet soda and pour some vodka in it. I'd chug it and use some mouthwash before going back in. It never affected me work wise, but I was losing control more than ever.

When I discovered the book *The Secret*, everything started slowly falling into place for me as I shifted my mindset. If you are not familiar with this book, it is a collection of thoughts and insights from some of the greatest minds in the world put together by an amazing woman named Rhonda Byrne. It truly changed my life forever and opened my mind to a whole new world that has endless possibilities! I am honored to be in Rhonda's new book *How 'The Secret' Changed My Life*! It features 70 stories of how *The Secret* changed people's lives, including mine. Thank you again, Rhonda!

I had stopped drinking every day and had returned to wrestling. I started seeing alcohol not as an aid to make me happy, but as something that was holding me back. When I was resigned to the WWE, I stopped cold turkey. I went three months with no alcohol and regained control over my life. Ever since, I have been able to drink or not drink. I give a lot of the credit for my ability to overcome my addiction to Holosync meditation, which has been proven to strengthen the prefrontal cortex, the part of the brain that regulates addiction. I have done it and truly believe it works. If you have tried everything and truly don't think there is anything else left, please try Holosync Meditation by Bill Harris.

Another addiction of mine early on in my wrestling career was something known as GHB (gamma-hydroxybutyric acid). For those of you who have never heard of GHB, it is a clear liquid that looks like water, but is usually thicker and has a horrible taste. It was once sold over the counter in supplement stores as a nighttime sleep aid. Eventually, though, the horror stories started coming out of people overdosing and being rushed to the hospital, people getting in car wrecks, and people dying. Taken in small amounts (a bottle cap's worth), it makes you feel drunk, but more relaxed and euphoric. When taken before bed, you sleep very deeply and often wake up in three to four hours very well rested. When you take too much, though, it is the absolute worst thing in the world and many people have died from GHB overdose. It is illegal and getting caught with it can ruin your life. When I was 23 years old and just starting my journey as a pro wrestler, I started taking this stuff multiple times a day. I used it as a crutch for relaxing and convinced myself that I needed it to survive the boot camp training school I was in. I took it after wrestling practice, again before the gym, and then again before bed every night for nearly a year. I would use it when we would go out for beers and was truly addicted to how it made me feel. I had many horrible moments on it, but the one that changed my life forever was the night I took it while drinking heavily. I almost died. It was an experience I will never forget and I never took it again. I was not nearly as developed mentally as I am today, but almost dying is enough to kick an addiction on the spot!

It is important for us to understand ourselves and realize where our addictions come from and what is triggering them in the first place. Once we understand that part of ourselves better, it can help us address our personal issues with the addiction. I had no idea what I was doing with my life during my GHB phase. If I had had goals and reasons for my existence, this sort of stuff wouldn't have been an issue for me. There is always a way out, but you have to find it from within. Nobody else can do that for you.

PERFORMANCE ENHANCING DRUGS

Performance enhancing drugs (PED) are a widespread problem on a worldwide scale. (I am talking about abusing steroids and not legit doctor-approved testosterone replacement therapy programs, which I will speak on further down.) They are tested for in every major professional sport and it is a constant game of cat and mouse. And while they might not be as bad as certain media outlets and publications over the years have made them out to be, they aren't ideal for an overall healthy lifestyle. I feel it is a person's choice whether or not they want to put something in their body, so this isn't about casting stones or being judgmental. Rather, it is about creating awareness. When it comes to sporting events and athletic competitions, I fully endorse drug testing, as it is absolutely necessary for creating a level playing field.

We need to continue to educate our youth and the world so that they know that while some of these steroids were legal at one time, not much was known about them. We have enough information now and should do all we can to eliminate these chemicals, as they aren't conducive to a long healthy life. I used them for a portion of my life and have seen firsthand what they can do, so I know we would be better off without them. A lot of active athletes don't like to talk about this, but I believe in being honest and learning from each other, so I am happy to share my experiences. Never in a million years would I have thought I would be someone who used steroids, but it happened and I learned a lifetime of valuable lessons from it. If it can help one kid make better choices, it is worth it.

I became obsessed with muscles and working out at a very young age. I remember being twelve years old and staying up at night doing push-ups, crunches, squats, and anything else I could do to build up my muscles. In high school I got put in the advanced weight training class a year before I should have technically started, but the coaches felt I belonged there and obviously so did I. I loved training and after several months in there, accusations of me being on steroids became a regular thing. I always laughed and thought it was a great compliment at the time because I had no clue about steroids. I have always had a great natural base and when you add an obsessive work ethic to that, it creates great results.

In college, I worked part time at a Gold's Gym and this is where I would learn about steroids. I would see larger-than-life pro bodybuilders come in all the time and often they would ask me if I wanted to compete. When a pro bodybuilder told me I had great genetics (I was 240 pounds naturally at the time), that triggered me to start reading up on steroids. I had always wanted to be a professional wrestler as a kid, but I didn't think it was a realistic goal. It just seemed like a fantasy. But when I saw how successful these guys at the gym had been using steroids, I thought maybe this was the way to make that dream come true. After a couple mild steroid cycles, I went from 240 pounds to 280 plus pounds in quite a short period of time. But my natural testosterone production was hit hard and would never be the same, since I was only 20 years old when I started. Looking back, I wish I had never started, but I had assumed that I needed to if I wanted to make it in wrestling, as the top people were using these things. That was a very immature mindset.

Very early into my wrestling career, the WWE began drug testing its performers and to this day, I am very thankful they took this approach. If they hadn't, there would be an even longer list of pro wrestlers found dead. After having done a few steroid cycles very early in my life, I was very happy to be done with it when the WWE introduced their drug-testing program. I take great pride in my physique and the work that goes into staying the size that I am. Whenever I hear people accuse me of still using steroids, it lets me know my hard work is working. I would never pass judgment on anyone for choices they make, as it isn't my business, but hopefully we can continue to educate ourselves and our youth that amazing results can be achieved through hard work and a solid game plan.

We are still so close to the so-called steroid era of the 70s, and a lot of people think it is taking a step backwards to stop using steroids now that we know what people can look like and do while on these substances. But these things are not what we once thought, and we are better off not using them and not having access to them outside of medicinal purposes. I understand that a lot of people who still partake in this lifestyle may be upset at my words, but deep down we all know it to be true. The side effects just aren't worth it. The human body is capable of looking amazing without steroids and it will just take time for us as a society to adjust. I recently had a grown man come up to me in the gym and ask for my opinion. He proceeded to tell me he had been using steroids for some time and was 90 pounds over his natural limit. He had been on a cycle of steroids for some time and had a cough that wouldn't go away. The results of blood work he'd recently had done were very bad. His liver and kidney values, cholesterol, and several other important things were way above the normal range, and he also had high blood pressure. He was honest with his doctor, and his doctor told him the results were the way they were because of all the steroids. This man looked at me and said, "I don't think it is the steroids." I told him that I believe there is a very good chance it is because of the steroids, and that he needs to come off of everything long enough to let his body normalize and then go back in for further blood work. I told him that when we are doing something we know deep down is bad for us, we will justify it by lying to ourselves. I know this because that is what I did with nicotine and steroids in my early 20s. He said he needed the steroids to be big, so I told him he didn't need them to be big and that the reason many people use them is because they let others who have used them influence their judgment of themselves. He thanked me and assured me he was going to stop and get further blood work, and I truly hope he did. There are plenty of healthier ways to enhance the body that don't put our health at risk. WWE is now utilizing guys who are smaller than the guys of the past and conditioning the audience that they are the future, and I totally get it from a business standpoint. Guys like me are few and far between, though, and I feel they will see moving forward that a guy who can naturally be 280 pounds at 6'2" and stay healthy and work with anyone isn't something you see every day.

None of what I have been talking about so far relates to testosterone replacement therapy (TRT), which is done for medical purposes. Many men truly suffer from having low testosterone, and it is no laughing matter. The side effects of having low T can be just as bad if not worse than having high testosterone. A doctor will determine through blood-work if a man's body is producing enough natural testosterone and then prescribe testosterone if it isn't. The dose is usually between 75 to 150 mg a week and is available in different delivery forms (injection, gels, creams, etc.). Men are also usually prescribed human chorionic gonadotropin or HCG to keep their testicles working just enough so that they remain normal sized and intact during the duration of the treatment. Typically, this treatment is for men who are done having kids and for whom nothing else has worked. It has helped millions of men live healthier, improved lives and definitely serves its purpose well. I started TRT at the early age of 29. After having low testosterone for five years, I felt I had no choice. I put my job first and felt that balanced testosterone levels were necessary for optimal health and for me to fully take advantage of my time on the road. It wasn't until after starting the TRT that I realized just how bad I had felt prior. I did eventually come off TRT, taking a chance to regain my natural testosterone. It was an exciting challenge. One of the biggest reasons I wanted to do it was because I was starting Feed Me More Nutrition and having my very own natural testosterone booster was very important to me. I researched natural herbs for years and finally found the right mixture and ingredients, and they restored my natural testosterone for the first time in over ten years. If you are interested in learning more, go to feedmemore.com and check out "The Big Guy" Testosterone Booster. I have been passionate about supplements since I was a kid, and I take great pride in having my own line. A lot of today's products are endorsed by people who use PEDs, and while they look absolutely huge and shredded, they didn't get that way through proper supplementation alone. I will never judge the life of others, but I believe in being honest and letting others decide if that is the message they want their kids to follow. Feed Me More Nutrition will have my heart and soul in it because I believe in what I do and want kids and adults to have healthy options when it comes to supplementation. The only way we can change the way people think and act in the future is to start doing it now.

Another thing coming to the forefront is human growth hormone. It is only a matter of time before this is tested for all the time and certain organizations such as the Olympics have already begun. The testing is very expensive, but hopefully over time that cost comes down and the test is more accessible. Human growth hormone doesn't shut the body down like steroids and when used under a doctor's supervision has its place, but like steroids, it can be abused. While I personally don't think the side effects are as bad as steroids, it is a performance-enhancing drug. We have to get away from the mindset that this stuff is commonplace and acceptable. Athletes are always going to push themselves to do whatever it takes to win, so we must continue to educate and make the penalties severe enough that others won't want to make the same mistake.

Elite athletes are elite athletes because of their minds, first and foremost, and that will never change. Maybe guys won't be quite as big and ripped without performance-enhancing drugs, but they can still look amazing. There are plenty of natural ingredients that do not affect our health like steroids and other PEDs do, and we must get away from this mindset that we need them to perform at a certain level. We are meant to evolve as a species and make things better for the next generation. We need to help our children develop a new mindset about this as they grow up.

Section 2

INSPIRATION AND ATTITUDE

BEING THANKFUL

Being grateful or thankful is something you hear a lot of people talk about these days. We all pay attention to being thankful during the American holiday of Thanksgiving (a favorite holiday of yours truly, by the way), but I think we should be taught to be thankful each and every moment of our lives. Again, it was the book *The Secret* that brought this idea to my attention. I didn't truly grasp this concept right away because I had a lot of negativity in my mind and my life when I first came across that book. Over time, though, as I gained control over my thoughts and managed the negativity in my life, I slowly started becoming more thankful for the people around me and the things in my life. Another book from the creators of *The Secret*, called *The Magic*, focuses solely on being thankful and the power gratitude can have on your life. It takes you step by step and includes exercises and daily tasks for applying gratitude to your life. By the time you are done with the book, being thankful is instinctual. It is just so powerful when you can be truly thankful for things. Every day of life is a gift and we must understand this and cherish this mindset. I personally try to say thank you from morning to night, and though there are times I forget, I am light years ahead of where I was years ago. It starts when my eyes open in the morning and I say thank you for the great day that awaits me. From there I say thank you for the water I drink upon wakening and any food I eat throughout the day, remembering the lives that were sacrificed for my meal. When I'm listening to a song I love, I say thank you for allowing me to hear this music and thank you for the artists who dedicated their lives to their passion. I do this for many different things in my day until I lay down in bed, where I say thank you for this comfortable bed and another great day of life. I will bet this seems excessive, as when I first read of people doing this, it seemed impossible to be this thankful! I assure you it is simply a shift in your mindset and you will begin doing it more and more. It is effortless when you are truly thankful, so simply feel it, and watch the way it can transform your life.

Having several serious injuries during my time in WWE allowed me to truly understand what being thankful for my health means. When you go from seemingly being able to do anything to being laid up in bed, it gives you a lot of time to think. It was during a shoulder injury in my time in developmental that I discovered the book *Think and Grow Rich* by Napoleon Hill. A great quote by Napoleon that changed the way I thought and meditated was, "If you make your prayers an expression of gratitude and thanksgiving for the blessings you have already received, instead of requests for what you do not have, you will obtain results a great deal faster." Looking back, I always used to beg and ask for things that I didn't have when I prayed. It never worked. This quote shifted my mindset to being grateful for what I already had, rather than focusing so much on what I didn't have. I read Hill's book after *The Secret* and it took me to another level. Looking back, I see that gratitude was one of the final pieces of the puzzle in my life that didn't come right away from reading *The Secret*. Sure, I said thank you at times, but truly feeling thankful and recognizing just how amazing every moment of life truly is didn't come until much later. Try to get in the habit of saying thank you to other people and for the things you come in contact with, and I assure you it will improve the quality of your life! I will leave you with this quote on gratitude from Zig Ziglar, as it has always resonated well with me: "Gratitude is the healthiest of all human emotions. The more you express gratitude for what you have, the more likely you will have even more to express gratitude for."

Things to be thankful for:-

Napoleon Hill

INSPIRATIONAL QUOTES

Throughout my house, there are many posters with inspirational quotes. I felt the need to share these quotes because they have helped me tremendously. They come from people who have achieved great things in life, so practicing their wisdom definitely couldn't hurt, right? The best thing about inspirational quotes is that people can interpret them however they see fit. I will explain how I interpret each one, but your interpretation may be different.

"The journey of a thousand miles begins with a single step." – Lao Tzu

I interpret this to mean that everything we do begins with taking that first step towards our goals and committing. Sometimes the end result seems so far away or impossible, but if we just chip away at our goals and do a little each day, the results will be dramatic. We just have to get off our asses and take the first step, as that is often the most difficult one to take.

"It's not the hours you put in, it's what you put in the hours." – Sam Ewing

This is pretty straightforward: put in the work and bust your ass! Don't waste time and brag that you worked for twelve hours when you half-assed it and could have accomplished those tasks in three hours. It is about making the most of each and every minute, hour, day, week, month, and year and living our lives to our maximum capacity. It is about believing that no matter how much time we have, we are going to do what it takes to succeed.

"Going one more round when you don't think you can, that's what makes all the difference in your life." – Rocky Balboa

This amazing quote from the legendary Rocky movie is something that helped me so much with wrestling and life. When we get that feeling of wanting to quit because we are so physically or mentally tired, we have to dig deep down inside ourselves and find a way to push even harder! It inspired the phrase "Finish It" that I used in my matches. It is about squeezing out a few more reps when you think you have nothing left in the tank. The human mind is very special and when we tap into its powers, there is nothing we can't do if we just have heart and passion.

> *"Life begets life. Energy creates energy. It is by spending oneself that one becomes rich."* – Sarah Bernhardt

When I first saw this quote, I absolutely fell in love with it and bought the poster, framed it, and hung it in my house. Just reading it is empowering! I take it to mean that what you put into your life, life gives back to you. If you work hard and spend yourself each and every day, you can have and be whatever you believe. This is one of my all-time favorite quotes and I will forever hold this close to my heart.

> *"The worst thing I could be is the same as everybody else. I'd hate that."* – Arnold Schwarzenegger

Arnold has played a huge role in my life and meeting him years ago was such a great experience. He is the epitome of hard work and dedication. This quote is simple—he was never going to settle for average. I am not saying that being average is bad, because it isn't, but if you want to be your best and strive for the impossible, this quote will empower you. It hangs in my bedroom and every time I see it, I just smile and nod my head as if Arnold is looking at me himself and saying this.

> *"I swing big, with everything I've got. I hit big or I miss big. I like to live as big as I can."* – Babe Ruth

I love Babe Ruth, coming from a baseball family myself. Life is about taking chances and that is what I get from this. It is about not being afraid to go for it when you believe in yourself and enjoying this beautiful and amazing thing we call life.

> *"Never let the fear of striking out get in your way."* – Babe Ruth

Another great quote by "The Babe" that hangs proudly in my house. Don't be afraid to go for it all! Don't let the fear of failure dictate your life. You can apply this to any aspect of your life and if we all could think like this man more often, fear wouldn't be nearly as prevalent.

> *"Keep your eyes on the stars, and your feet on the ground."* – Theodore Roosevelt

I love this quote and will always have this mentality. It means stay grounded and never let your ego get out of control. Stand up for yourself if people are being rude or disrespectful or walking all over you, but be a good person. It always makes me happy when I meet someone new and after just hanging out and talking, they tell me I seem so normal. It is because money and fame are just a result of my hard work and that is where it ends for me. Just keep your ego in check at all times because it only takes once for it to have serious consequences.

> *"The people who are crazy enough to think they can change the world are the ones who do."* – Steve Jobs

Steve Jobs had an incredible mind and his contributions to this world were incredible. Don't be afraid to dream big and do things nobody else thinks is possible. All that matters is if you believe it is possible. Before I made it in wrestling, I hung a check on my wall for 1 million dollars because that seemed like a lot of money to me at that time (it still seems like a lot of money). Whenever other people would see it, they would laugh. I never minded it and I could understand the humor in it, but it didn't stop me from making that amount my first year on a full-time WWE schedule (a feat very few accomplish). Steve Jobs understood life and if you can think even a little like him, your life can't help but improve!

> *"It is never too late to be what you might have been."* – George Eliot

The moment I saw this quote I had to have it for my house and now it proudly hangs in my kitchen. I had never learned back flips as a kid and never thought I could do it. At 35 years old, after seeing this quote, I said to myself, "I can do this," and I went and learned how to do a backflip in one hour! I have kept this quote close to me and applied it to so many new things I have always wanted to do, but just figured it was too late. It is never too late! That is all you need to get from this quote. It will give you a sense of freedom knowing anything is still possible in life, no matter what your age is.

"The difference between try and triumph is a little umph." – Marvin Phillips

Truer words have never been said. It is the difference between being good and being great at something. It means putting in the work and effort can make all the difference. This poster hangs in my bedroom and always replays in my mind when I need it most.

"I'm a great believer in luck, and I find the harder I work the more I have of it." – Thomas Jefferson

There are quite a few different versions of this quote and I love all of them! Essentially, it means that great things happen for people who work hard and prepare. While it may appear from the outside that they are just lucky, it is what they are doing behind the scenes that sets them up for success. Luck is a very real thing, but it gets more credit than it deserves most of the time.

"A person who won't read has no advantage over one who can't read." – Mark Twain

Being an avid reader and listener of audio books, this one really hits home. Reading has allowed me to learn about so many amazing things and apply them to my life and has played a huge part in my decision to write my first book. Reading to educate ourselves is one of the greatest things we could ever do for ourselves. Mr. Twain clearly knew this.

"People might not get all they work for in this world, but they must certainly work for all they get." – Frederick Douglass

This great quote hangs just outside my bedroom and I read it daily when home. I take this to mean you have to put in the hard work and bust your ass for your goals. You may not get exactly what you were looking for out of that hard work, but you will be far better off for doing it. Life isn't always fair, but that cannot stop us from doing our best at all times.

"Success is not the key to happiness. Happiness is the key to success." – Albert Schweitzer

This one is something I have more personal experience with than any other quote. I had a lot of success and made a lot of money with wrestling, but the lifestyle and the company I worked for made me absolutely miserable over a long period of time. I was living out of a different hotel room every night, driving in rental cars for hours on end, and living the same routine day in and day out. And no matter how hard I worked or applied myself, those efforts weren't recognized or rewarded. Instead, I was punished and lied to time and time again. No amount of money could make up for my unhappiness, so I made a life-altering decision to say no more. I now have a chance to live my life and be rewarded for my efforts. We have to choose happiness over anything else in life, along with love, as success alone cannot guarantee that. Love what you do and love yourself and you cannot go wrong.

> *"Live as if you were to die tomorrow. Learn as if you were to live forever."* – Mahatma Gandhi

This quote really hits home with me and is a staple in my home. What a great way to approach life. Educate yourself and learn as much as you can every single day, but don't be afraid to actually LIVE life!

> *"Darkness cannot drive out darkness; only light can do that. Hate cannot drive out hate; only love can do that."* – Dr. Martin Luther King

In a world filled with so much hate and violence, I love reading this quote, and I try to apply it to my life whenever I can. I am not perfect and have not always lived by this, but I feel it has helped me when I needed it most. This doesn't mean you have to let people use you or walk all over you. But there is always a way to fight back without violence if we use our minds, and Mr. King will forever live on for his efforts. He was blessed with a truly beautiful mind.

> *"Thousands of candles can be lighted from a single candle, and the life of the candle will not be shortened. Happiness never decreases by being shared."* – Buddha

Just be a good person whenever you can. We are all going to encounter rude, miserable, and ignorant human beings throughout our lives, but let's try our best not to feed into their negativity. A simple smile to one stranger could change their entire day and the chain effect that could cause is enormous. Have you ever noticed how great you feel when you are good to people? Being rude to people doesn't feel good even if they deserve it. If you encounter negative people, just get away from them and don't sink to their level. Smile, be happy, and spread that happiness when you can because the world is a better place when the scales are tilted in favor of love and happiness.

> *"Pain is temporary. It may last a minute, or an hour, or a day, or a year, but eventually it will subside and something else will take its place. If I quit, however, it lasts forever."* – Lance Armstrong

I have found that there is a reason very few people ever make it to an elite level in their selected field or sport—success doesn't always show up right away and people often give up right before their big break. I know from experience that pushing yourself physically hurts and making it to a level where fame is involved requires a high threshold for criticism. The important thing is to set a goal, work hard to reach it, and stay hungry for it the entire time. Enjoy the ride, as the satisfaction of reaching it will be well worth it. We can all do great things, but if we quit, we don't even give ourselves the chance.

"Feed Me More" – The Big Guy Ryback

Now I can't do a chapter on inspirational quotes and not include mine! "Feed me more" is how I live my life. It is about waking up hungry and setting goals. It is about staying hungry day in and day out until you reach those goals. Once you reach those goals, it is about being and feeling thankful, but not becoming complacent. When the time is right and you are ready for more, you look to the universe and say, "Feed me more!" That is what "feed me more" means to me. Successful people are always hungry. What are you?

AIRPLANES AND ATTITUDE

I am beyond thankful that we can travel the world with relative ease. Technology continues to improve and our ability to move at rapid speeds in a safe and effective manner is at an all-time high. With that said, I find being in airports one of the most stressful things I deal with, but a lot of it can be avoided if handled properly. Being a professional wrestler requires you to fly several times a week, so I thought I'd share my experiences and some things that have helped me.

The recommended guideline we always hear is to get to an airport two hours early and that is usually more than enough time. If you want to shorten that time, I recommend signing up for TSA PreCheck if it's available at your location. It is never as crowded as the regular lines and can help alleviate a lot of unwanted stress. If you notice screening personnel not doing their jobs, as I sometimes do, call the airport administration to report the problem to help streamline this process for everyone.

Boarding the plane is another process that takes time. Getting status is key for making sure you can board in the first couple of groups and get yourself situated. During the flight, don't jack your seat back as fast as you can. Airplanes are only so big and you never know what the person behind you is doing or how crammed in they are. And carry a pair of noise-blocking headphones to save the day when a young one is crying in the seat next to you!

When you land, it is important to be patient so everyone can get off the plane efficiently. There is an unwritten rule that when exiting a plane you let the row ahead of you get out first. It doesn't matter if you have your stuff ready and the guy in front of you had a window seat. You give him time to exit and gather his stuff unless he gives you the nod to move ahead. When people don't adhere to this, it only makes things worse. Another strategy that has worked well to help me stay patient during deplaning is to stay occupied once the plane lands. I always gather my belongings to speed up the time it will take me to exit, but once I do that, I read, listen to an audio book, or stay busy on my phone. Sitting and staring as row after row gathers their stuff only seems to make the process that much longer. Doing all of these things can greatly improve your chances of avoiding unwanted stress while traveling.

AFFIRMATIONS

Affirmations were first introduced to me when I came across the book *The Secret*. Now I am sure I had heard of them before and possibly even used them from time to time, but I was unaware of how powerful they could be when used properly. An affirmation is the action or process of affirming something. An example is saying something to yourself such as, "Today I am going to have a great day and do my best at everything I do!" Affirmations can have such a powerful and positive influence on your life if you allow them to. But you must believe what you are saying in your affirmations to truly reap the benefits. When using affirmations, I like to use the words *I am, I am becoming*, and *I am committed to being*, such as, "I am the best version of myself today!" Or "I am becoming the best version of myself today!" and "I am committed to being the best version of myself today!" I use affirmations when I meditate and again at night before bed. If there is a big wrestling event or I am speaking in front of a large group of people, I will use affirmations before stepping in the ring or on stage. Affirmations can help create a great sense of confidence and have had a tremendous impact on my life. The affirmations I repeat daily to myself are " I am whole, I am perfect, I am strong, I am powerful, I am loving, I am harmonious, I am happy, I am healthy, I am committed to being my best, I am ultra rich, I am compassionate, I am giving, I am confident, I am courageous, I am the greatest big guy in the universe, my inner world creates my outer world, and I am committed to bettering myself each and every day!" I say these affirmations with 100 percent commitment and belief and do my best to feel each one as I speak it. I also include what I am thankful for. Simply doing the "I am whole, perfect, strong, powerful, loving, harmonious, happy, and healthy" routine is a great way to start getting accustomed to affirmations. I truly feel if you allow positive affirmations into your life that you too can experience the benefits that I have!

FEAR OF FAILURE AND CRITICISM

The fear of failure is something I knew very well many years ago. It is quite possibly the single biggest factor in people not accomplishing what they want. It causes people to make excuses, lie to themselves, and try to convince others that they would have been if not for (insert any possible reason here). It can cause us to sit on our hands and watch the world pass us by. For me, the fear of failure really kicked in during my first year wrestling at Deep South Wrestling. I became afraid to try and to work on new things. I became afraid to trust my instincts. I was afraid of what people might say or that they would critique me and make me feel bad. When they did, I let it bring me down. I say this now with a smile on my face, but it fucking ate me alive for a long time that I let other people influence *my life*. It took getting fired from wrestling for a couple years for me to rediscover myself and learn not to let the fear of failure and criticism bring me down. I accepted that fear was controlling my life and that it was ok to recognize the fear, but then it was up to me to act accordingly and not let it defeat me!

To this very day, whenever I feel the fear of failure and criticism creep into my mind, I know that I need to go do whatever it is I want to do and put that fear to rest. A couple years ago, I really wanted to learn about guns and to start investing in guns for home security. I felt that fear creep in, worrying that they would think the almighty Ryback was clueless about guns. Of course I was. I had never learned about them. I knew what I had to do, so I went into a local gun shop. The guys behind the counter knew me instantly, and I just said, "Guys, I don't know a thing about guns. Can you help me learn?" Right then and there, the fear died and I made my purchases. When I picked them up several days later, I went straight to a gun range and again informed them I was clueless about guns and would like to learn how to shoot. They kindly helped me feel comfortable and instructed me on the range safety rules and regulations.

I now swing by there from time to time to fire off some of my guns and it is something I truly enjoy.

Another situation I found myself in a while back was that I wanted to be able to do a back flip, something I had never learned to do, as I mentioned in the Inspirational Quotes section. I had always wanted to be able to do standing back flip splashes and moonsaults in the wrestling ring, but without learning how to perform a back flip, that wasn't going to happen. One day while home off the road, I just said, "Screw it, I want to learn this now!" I looked up a local gymnastics studio and drove down. The girl at the front charged me twenty dollars and I was free to go practice . As I walked in, I saw some instructors, loads of kids, and parents watching their kids. I was filled with the fear that everyone was going to judge me and laugh at me for trying to learn how to back flip. The kids in the class were very good and I just wanted to go home. The moment that feeling hit me, I said no way! I went out there and had an instructor help me and after 45 minutes—bam!—I did my first real back flip! Like a kid, I just kept doing them over and over and after an hour, I was covered in sweat and filled with pure joy. Had I let the fear of failure and criticism control me, I never would have experienced the overwhelming sense of joy when I was able to learn something that had eluded me for so long.

Just because you have never done something before doesn't mean that you should never try and learn. Most of us suck at things we have never done and it takes getting over that initial hump to get a little confidence in something. Don't worry about the negativity from other people. Know who you are and what you ultimately want, and I assure you that you will be able to control the fear of failure and criticism rather than allowing it to control you.

COMPETING WITH OURSELVES

I cannot stress enough how competitive I am and how I always want to be my best at everything. It has brought me a tremendous amount of success, but also a good amount of unwanted stress. When we are young, we are taught that when we are better at something than someone else, we get first prize or we get the biggest trophy or we are perceived as a winner, and that is all great. What tends not to be taught is that losing is a part of life and that even if we aren't the winner or the best, that doesn't make us a loser or not *our* best. I think being competitive brings out the best in all of us, but just like any other aspect of life, it can become an unhealthy obsession or addiction if not carefully controlled. Ultimately, I feel we need to teach our youth from the beginning that competition is about being our absolute best. We all have different backgrounds and starting points in life and there is always going to be someone who is bigger, stronger, faster, tougher, prettier, leaner, taller, or any other adjective of your choice on any given day. Life is about the journey and the moments and emotions that come with that journey. Competing with others is great and can be so much fun, but it is important to understand that, first and foremost, we are competing with ourselves. Whether you are an aspiring bodybuilder looking to do your first bodybuilding show, a white belt jiujitsu student entering your first tournament, or a kid playing a team sport for the first time, it is the journey and being *your* best that ultimately is what you are after. It requires a very mature mindset to think this way and fully understand it. When you fully grasp this, you may not be overly thrilled you came in second place or came out on the losing end in a game, but you will have a sense of pride and happiness that you gave it your all and on that particular day were *your* best. You will often hear people complain (people love to complain these days) that we are celebrating losing by handing out awards to all participants, but that has nothing to do with what I am talking about. If people understood this state of mind better, we wouldn't have to create trophies for everyone to make them feel good. They would just feel good knowing they did their best. I am talking about a mature state of mind that, along with a positive attitude towards life, will make our lives better. Remember, there is no right or wrong, only what we believe, and I believe that if we can master competing with ourselves, we will have mastered a very important part of life!

LIFE VALUES

Many years ago, at the beginning of my journey of self-improvement, I came along what I would call a golden nugget. A golden nugget is a piece of information in a book that I retain and apply to my life. If I just get one golden nugget from a book, it was well worth my time. Even if you just read one book a year and get one golden nugget a year, just think how that could positively affect your life if applied.

So this golden nugget I speak of came from a great Tony Robbins book called *Unlimited Power*. He spoke about something called life values. Essentially, it is a list or vision board of why we live our lives. Why do we wake up each and every day and do what we do? Well, if we have our life values in order, we do the things we do to enhance our lives for ourselves and those around us. Many people have no clue why they do what they do and, with that mindset, you greatly increase your chances of making bad decisions or doing things that aren't in your best interest. I challenge you to sit down and write out your top five life values and then look at what you are doing and how you can improve the things in your life to line up with those values. Number one should be your absolute number one reason for living and then you go from there. So for example, my number one life value is health because I cannot live the life I want to live without my health. I have listed my top five life values and why I do what I do in my life below.

Also, there is nothing wrong with having ten life values or fifteen. I am just using five for this book as I feel if we all have five, we have our core in place to live a healthy productive life.

1. Health
2. Happiness
3. Love
4. Money

5. Power

As I explained above, I can't live the life I want to live without good health. Following health is happiness. What is the point of living an unhappy life? What we do should make us happy, the people around us should make us happy, and the places we choose to go should make us happy. I don't know about everyone else, but I don't wake up to be miserable! Coming in at number three for me is love. Love of oneself, family, and friends. Love is the most powerful form of energy in the universe. You can have all the wealth and possessions in the world, but if you lack health, happiness, and love, what is the point? Number four for me is money because I truly believe we are meant to have whatever we want in life if we are willing to work for it and believe in it. The world we live in is built around money and it allows us to do and have the things we want. It helps us in emergencies and can help give our families better security. Number five for me is power, by which I mean power for good. To be able to influence people and the world, you need the power to spread your message and help add value to people's lives.

Every single life value is important and the ones at the top of the list reinforce the ones that come after. Go out and buy a vision board, write down your life values, and start getting closer to your goals! You cannot get to where you are going without a final destination in mind. I hope this has helped you and I look forward to hearing your life values.

SOCIETY TODAY

It is so frustrating to sit here in 2016 and see the problems our country is experiencing. Because anyone can post to social media and upload edited videos to display whatever message they are trying to get across, we have more hate than ever being passed from person to person. We are slowly creating a war within our own country over incidents that have nothing to do with the majority of us. Our world isn't perfect and the structure we currently live in isn't perfect, but we have got to be smarter in how we react to and handle situations.

Bitching and moaning and creating more hate online over things that aren't even being portrayed accurately isn't helping solve anything. People murdering police officers who have nothing to do with other isolated incidents isn't solving the problem. While not every police officer is great, the vast majority are, and they have dedicated their lives to making ours better. Ultimately, everything they enforce is for our safety and while we may not always agree with them, we should always respect them. Bad things happen in life and if we react to those bad situations with more bad, we are only adding fuel to the fire. It absolutely sucks racism exists in 2016, but by protesting with violence or by destroying parts of your own city, you are doing absolutely nothing to solve the problem. Protesting in highways and disrupting traffic and putting good people just trying to get home to their families in jeopardy is absolutely not called for and is unacceptable. We have to be smarter than this and we have to start being accountable for ourselves. Most people just like jumping on the bandwagon and are complaining for the sake of complaining. They don't actually sit back and analyze things from different perspectives. I have news for you people who love stirring things up—if you obey the law and just adhere to being a good person, more often than not, you will avoid problems with the law. Now, that isn't to say that something bad can't still happen, but it certainly decreases your chances.

We have to educate ourselves and be intelligent enough to know there are constructive ways to protest or raise awareness of issues. We must evolve if we are to continue to prosper as a country, let alone individuals. I love our country and the majority of the people in it, but we are letting the bad ones influence good people with their screwed-up ways and beliefs. Ultimately, it comes down to us as individuals taking care of ourselves and our families, and if we all could just do that, a lot of problems would take care of themselves. This is obviously much easier said than done. This isn't a time for us to try to separate ourselves and create more hate than already exists. We must love more than ever and try harder than we ever have to have an open heart and forgive. We can't just say that all cops are bad or all black people are bad or all white people are bad. The future of our country is in our hands and we have to handle it with care more than ever.

So let's spend less time watching bullshit Facebook videos and arguing with each other online and just love ourselves and the ones we care about most. That will do more good than you could possibly imagine. I believe if we all just focused on ourselves and our loved ones and quit trying to judge every other human being, some of these problems would improve. Let's be more focused on donating time to a local homeless shelter, giving the guy on the corner some money for a meal, or donating to a cause we fully support instead of being filled with so much hate and prejudice. People are so quick to throw stones and judge others rather than letting our system take care of the people who fall out of line. As far as I'm concerned, we are all human beings and we are one race. It is time for us to eliminate this bullshit and realize that those who came before us were fucking wrong. We are the generation to put an end to all this madness. The world was not created to be divided and fought over and there is more than enough for everyone. The best thing we can do is teach the people within our walls true love and let the hate die out over time.

Just look at our current presidential election. All the media does is look for negative ways to portray the men and women who ultimately want to make our country better. Of course politicians look out for themselves and their families in the process—EVERYONE SHOULD DO THAT. We are in such a negative, judgmental state that we let our opinions become filled with hate and vengeance. We look at other people and think, "Oh my God, you are voting for him?" or "You are voting for her?" and then we criticize and judge. A president won't fix all your problems. *You* are responsible for fixing your problems. It is just disheartening we cannot be more mature and responsible in 2016. Recently, I posted a picture on social media about a book I recommended about financial education written by Donald Trump and Robert Kiyosaki, and made no mention of anything related to presidential preference. The comments for the picture were filled with hate and negativity, not only towards Donald Trump, but also me, simply because I was sharing a good book that could help raise awareness about money. It starts with each and every one of us, and we cannot continue down this hate-filled path. Ultimately, I want to believe these people want to make our country as good as possible, because they too have family and loved ones that will have to survive long after they are gone. Change for the better is up to us, and it begins with adopting a more positive mindset towards all people. So smile more, judge less, and be happy now.

DESTRUCTIVE CRITICISM

From the moment we are born to the day we move on, there will be criticism. It seems the more well known someone becomes and the more successful they are, the greater the criticism. Some comes from peers and coworkers, while other criticism comes from critics who are paid to critique, even if they don't necessarily feel a certain way. Largely, though, the majority of criticism comes from those who have not found success or gotten their act together. A large portion of our world is unhappy and when they see others have success, the easy thing for them to do is be jealous and to use destructive criticism to try and make themselves feel better. I am not talking about constructive criticism from people who are trying to help and motivate you. I am focusing on destructive criticism. I don't know where it started, but human beings have become so judgmental about pretty much anything and everything. It seems nobody can do anything these days without a percentage of the population whining and crying and throwing insults. When you live your life watching others live their lives, that is usually what happens. Even if we are confident and positive, it still doesn't feel good to see people who don't know you say absurd things that they'd never have the courage to say in real life. The block and mute features on social media are a phenomenal tool to use to eliminate these negative people. It ultimately comes down to us having confidence in ourselves and knowing who we are. I believe life is an amazing beautiful experience and I look forward to continuously growing and learning and living life. Unfortunately, many people have not reached that mindset and have very negative feelings on life. I believe it all goes back to our media spreading this negativity at alarming rates and people's inability to learn new things that would allow them to break free from the limitations life in today's society can place on us.

The last seven years in wrestling have blown me away as some of our supposed fans have become some of the most outspoken critics. There are many great fans who appreciate everyone and enjoy it for what it is, but there is that negative part of the fan base that has lost all control. Again, I can't stress enough, you will rarely if ever see a successful, smart, educated person throwing destructive criticism around, especially in terms of social media. You know why? Because they realize how absurd it is and how much of a waste of energy it is, as well. Also, they are confident and most definitely believe in themselves. It is sad to see this destructive criticism because, for a lot of these people, there is no helping them and they will continue to live a life of unhappiness and negativity. Hopefully, if any of them come across this book, they can look in the mirror and start making some changes for themselves. If just one can do it then this section was worth it.

I can't tell you how many times I have received messages from fans telling me something positive and saying they want to like me, but they just can't. That's usually followed by an insult! It makes me laugh every time I see something like this and then shortly after my laughter, I block them and forever shut that person out of my world. Other times, there are the typical steroid accusations from people who don't work out or understand proper nutrition. There are also the people who try to insult me by saying I look like another wrestler or am ripping off this guy and impersonating that guy. Going even further, you have crazed fans who send death threats or wish harm upon you and your family. It is truly sad there aren't harsher ramifications for people who do this sort of thing. If there were serious penalties for people who threatened violence, I think it would help the problem. I remember being a kid and watching wrestling and loving it! I loved watching all the performers. Sure, I liked some more than others, but I never thought anyone sucked and if I'd had a way to communicate with them, the last thing on my mind would have been to insult them. How often do we see a movie that we think is bad or we don't like a character an actor played and then we hop on our phones and tweet them about how horrible of an actor they are and make a death threat? For me, never! Because anyone with half a brain realizes that is just idiotic. The point is that destructive criticism is all around us and we must remain strong and do our best to block it out and stay focused on what we are doing. Never let anyone discourage you from something that you want and believe in! If we did that, none of us would have anything in life. A positive mind stays on the grind, so block out the negativity and let's continue to keep living our lives how we see fit!

WE ALWAYS HAVE A CHOICE

I am a firm believer that we have more power inside us than we think and it is up to us to tap into that power. I believe our thoughts and beliefs attract to us people, places, and situations, but that sometimes things happen that we can't explain and we feel we have no control of. No matter what, though, we always have a choice in how we handle a particular situation. We get to choose whether we react in a positive or a negative way, whether we deal and move on or not. There have been many instances in my life where the situation seemed negative and bad, but I chose to believe and deal with it in a positive way, thus turning the event into a positive situation. One particular event was when I was 28 years old. I had gotten called up to WWE earlier that year from their developmental system, where I'd spent a few years trying several different characters. One character was Skip Sheffield, a corn-fed meathead from College Station, Texas. It couldn't have been any further from who I am as a person, but I love acting, so I submerged myself into this character and had an absolute blast just being stupid and making an ass of myself at times. Because this was the first time in my career I was actually having fun wrestling, I improved significantly and got called up to WWE TV. It was an amazing feeling and I really didn't want to believe there were any limitations on this character. Truth be told, though, a character like Skip Sheffield just wasn't the kind of act that becomes a superstar in the main event. And I had always believed that I would be—and was—a superstar.

After being on TV several weeks, I was informed by Vince McMahon that he wanted me to slowly ditch the act and take on an identity that was truer to my real personality. The perfect time for that came when seven other guys in the WWE and I formed a group called The Nexus. I just cranked up the intensity and aggression and ditched the hillbilly voice. People really took to the switch and our group was making major waves in the WWE. There was just one problem—I was stuck with this horrible name, Skip Sheffield! It had been fine before when that was what the character called for, but now it was an absolute curse and it really bothered me. I had used the name Ryback before Skip Sheffield, and I always wanted to be known by that name because it is a combination of my real name, Ryan, and Silverback, my nickname as a kid and my first wrestling name. All I could think about was changing to this name and getting good enough to be in the main events, doing what I knew I was capable of. One day we were performing a show in Hawaii, and I was involved in a tag team match, where there are two men in the ring and each man has a partner in the corner that they must tag in. Out of nowhere, I felt like my whole life flashed before my eyes and a force stronger than anything I could explain took over. A hot tag had taken place, where the two guys in the ring have tagged out at the same time and the good guys start mounting a comeback on the bad guys. At the time, I was playing the role of the bad guy with my partner and ran into a dropkick full speed. I wasn't supposed to fall down, as the comeback called for two dropkicks back to back, but on that first one, my left ankle rolled under, and my ankle broke in three places. I felt every one of them as I fell to the mat. To this day, I cannot tell you what possessed me to pop back up without blinking an eye, but I continued wrestling with one of WWE's best wrestlers, Tyson Kidd. We ended up doing all of the moves we had planned and didn't miss a beat. In fact, Tyson didn't even realize I was injured until he heard me grunt in pain after a move. He asked me if I was ok, and all I could do was mumble that I'd broken my ankle. We just kept going and every step I took in that ring after the initial break did more and more damage. With each step, the fractures in my ankle worked their way into my fibula, the bone in the side of your calf, and it broke all the way up to my knee! The finish of the match went down and after the 1-2-3, whatever energy had overtaken me to finish that match was gone, and I lay in the middle of that ring a mere mortal in excruciating pain. All I could think was that I had spent my entire adult life doing all I could to beat the odds and make it in the world of pro wrestling. Now I was freaking out that, in one moment, everything had come to a screeching halt and I might not get another chance. They rushed me to the hospital in Honolulu, drugged me up, put my ankle back into place, and casted it. They helped me back to my hotel and while everyone else went to Japan for a tour, I was on the next flight back to Tampa. On that airplane, I noticed a new book I had bought on the trip out to Hawaii.

It was none other than *The Power*, the sequel to the book *The Secret* that had been so influential in my wrestling career and life so far. Right then and there, it hit me that this was going to be the greatest thing that had ever happened to me. Never once did I doubt that this was the case, even though this would end up being one of the most trying and difficult times in my life, mentally and physically.

I will not go into all the messy details on the botched surgeries and the mind-blowing decisions made by key people whom I trusted to make sure I was properly taken care of. All I will say is, I had broken my bones, but I'd had no nerve damage or anything remotely close to that before the surgery. Afterwards, I had severe electrical shocks and pain. To this day, I still don't know how I coped with that for over six months. The surgeon had put a foot-long metal plate through my myofascial tissue and put two long screws through the perineal and superficial nerves in my leg. My nerves were screaming and firing for their lives, and I also had drop foot syndrome and lost full function of my left big toe, which to this day still hasn't come back. Through all of this, I had the belief that all these things were happening to me to keep me away from wrestling for a while so that I could come back as Ryback. Even in the most difficult of times, when it would have been easy to break down and just quit trying, not once did I ask, "Why me?" Deep down, I knew this was going to make me the man I needed to be in order to do what I wanted in this life. Several doctors told me my career as a wrestler would be over. They were clueless as to why I had lost function in my foot, and they said that walking and just living a normal life could be very difficult if this didn't improve soon.

The healing process took a year and a half, even though it should have taken no more than four to five months tops, but never did I believe my career was over. It was in this time I began the Holosync Meditation by Bill Harris. I reminded myself daily that my nerves were regenerating and I would have the most amazing comeback story. Eventually, because I felt I had to take control of the situation and top medical doctors seemed flabbergasted and couldn't decide what we should do next, I asked to have all the metal taken out of my leg from the first two surgeries. My nerves weren't dead yet and this metal was ruining my life. I wanted it out. They were hesitant at first, as they probably couldn't imagine that a doctor the WWE sent me to could cause this amount of damage. Sure enough, once the metal was removed, my suspicions were confirmed—the metal had been damaging my nerves. It would have been easy to feel sorry for myself and again react negatively, but I held to my belief that I would make this the best thing that had ever happened to me. Even the most negative situations can be reacted to positively. It sometimes doesn't happen right away, but all it takes is one moment to switch your mindset and start finding solutions where there don't appear to be any.

After the metal was removed, I felt an internal peace for the first time in fifteen months, and I knew I was going to do big things. I was able to find the positives in a situation that appeared to everyone else as a tragic negative. I can say with 100 percent certainty that if I had reacted negatively at any point in this process and had not woken up each day hungry to overcome this, my career would have been cut short, my nerves would have lost all function, and I most likely would have ended up in a wheelchair or using some sort of walking device for the rest of my life. This taught me such a valuable life lesson that I always go back to when things in my life aren't going as planned. Things happen to each and every one of us that we don't like or agree with and that is totally ok! Even if we initially react negatively to the situation, all it takes is one moment to change that. It isn't always easy when something happens that makes us angry or sad. Human emotions are very powerful forces. But if you continue to feel that way for a day, a week, a month, or even years, that is wasted energy that would be better spent focusing on solutions. None of us is perfect, so the best thing we can do is just remain conscious of our feelings moving forward and remember we always have a choice!

EGO IS OUR FRIEND AND ENEMY

Ego is defined by the dictionary as "a person's sense of self-esteem or self-importance." I think there is a very fine line between being highly confident and crossing that barrier into cockiness. We always hear star athletes or celebrities described as having overinflated egos, but I would never judge anyone based on someone else's words, especially that of the media. It is very important for us to understand the ego that lies inside each of us so we better understand ourselves and other people. The majority of people have an unhealthy belief in their own importance. They don't do it on purpose, but it's hard to see ourselves from an outside perspective.

I read a great book on ego recently called *Ego is the Enemy* by Ryan Holiday. In it, he says we should be humble in our aspirations, gracious in our success, and resilient in our failures, and I completely agree. Mr. Holiday also suggests we ask ourselves who we want to be and what path we want to take. I think we all should sit down by ourselves or with our family and loved ones and figure this out to give ourselves guidance and direction.

While an overinflated ego isn't good, we absolutely must love ourselves to be truly happy and to make those around us happy. I'm not talking about being narcissistic, but truly loving our human selves, mind, body, and soul and appreciating the amazing gift of life we get each day.

Early on in my life, I was very shy. I have always had a few close friends but have never had a lot of friends. I am, for the most part, what people would call a lone wolf. I have always been happy when alone, and I love to learn and reflect on life. I have actually made it a point to step out of my comfort zone and be more social in an attempt to broaden my horizons at this point in my life. When I got into wrestling, I realized I had to increase my confidence and how I carried myself. My first two years in wrestling, I was still very shy and let other people's opinions affect how I saw myself. In the wrestling world there is a small portion of the audience that are referred to as "smart marks" and some of them are some of the worst human beings I have ever encountered. Most wrestlers, celebrities, and athletes deal with our share of crazy fans. I have had people accuse me of having a huge ego and being rude and it just sucks. There was one time where a guy at an airport had fifteen trading cards he wanted signed so he could sell them on eBay, and I quite frankly didn't feel like signing that particular night as I was exhausted and had been traveling all day. I said, "No, thank you, buddy," as I always do when not in the mood, and this guy started screaming in the airport and followed me all the way out to my taxi. He later took to social media, declaring to the world how big my ego was and lying about what had happened. I've had quite a few encounters like this and it always hurts me. I have always believed in myself and while at times when younger I lacked the ability to show it, I always have known who and what I am. I love myself and I love good people. I want to help those who need help. But I refuse to ever let anyone walk all over me or unfairly criticize me when they have no business addressing anything other than themselves. I have always wanted to be famous and have power so I can have a mass influence worldwide, as I feel I can help make a positive difference through my life. So if there is anyone reading this who thinks I have a big ego, just know that yes, I believe in myself, because I know who and what I am in this life, but I assure you my ego is in check and it always will be.

Though it is a problem when people cross the fine line between confidence and arrogance, it is also a problem that many of us don't have enough confidence! I firmly believe learning to love ourselves and developing a trust and confidence in ourselves is absolutely vital if we are to grow and evolve. If we don't know our self-worth, we end up selling ourselves short and settling, thus missing out on some great things in life. Also, people who suffer from low confidence can sometimes mistake someone who is confident for someone who has an overinflated ego. They say, "If you don't believe in you, nobody else will believe in you," and I firmly believe this. We have to have a certain level of confidence and belief from within and have the courage and the strength to love ourselves like we were intended to. That doesn't mean constant bragging and showing off, but being proud of what you have done doesn't make you an egomaniac.

After I announced I was leaving WWE, I heard a small minority of people via social media say I had an out-of-control ego. But it isn't true. I just respected myself and my abilities too much to continue in a situation that was bad for me. I took control and will go create my own empire and world where my beliefs will allow me to prosper and not suffer. I feel that as long as we keep our confidence high but in check with humility and discipline, we allow ourselves the greatest balance and never go too far past that fine line. I think teaching our youth about ego and keeping it in check is extremely important as it will help suppress egos early on before bad habits can take control.

FORGIVENESS

We have all held hate inside our minds, bodies, and hearts. It is something I have done in my life, even after becoming more aware and adding things like positive thinking and meditation into my daily regimen. It isn't hard to let this happen when something affects us personally. It is hard to accept that other people could do things to hurt us or cause us pain, but as humans, every single one of us has hurt someone at one point or another. I have held hate for others inside for far too long before finally realizing that I had to let go of that emotion and forgive and move on. Holding hate inside negatively affects my life and, quite honestly, isn't worth it. I have learned to take a deep breath and try my best to put myself in the other person's shoes and situation. Holding in hate can have many different negative effects on us, according to medical researchers, as listed here by Valueoptions.com:

- elevated blood pressure
- increased heart rate
- tense muscles
- heart attack
- hiatal hernia
- glaucoma
- stroke
- hives
- asthma
- ulcers
- migraines
- low back pain
- psoriasis
- shortened life expectancy

Those of us who hold in anger and hate end up showing it in a variety of ways. It isn't uncommon for people who hold in these negative emotions to be overly critical, judgmental, or depressed. As someone who has been on television, I try to understand the people who use social media in a negative way. The world can be a rough place if we let it dictate our emotions, and I understand there are a lot of very miserable people out there. That is why I feel it is important for us to try and understand ourselves and our emotions better, so we can better ourselves and those we love. Anger and hate can impact us in every area of our lives, and we may not even realize it. Ignoring our feelings and why they exist isn't acceptable. It is up to us to dive deep into our minds and try to sort things out. The best way to start this process is to first accept forgiveness and then apply it to others so we can move on and be truly happy. Wayne Dyer, a world-renowned author, sums it up best when he says, "Your life is like a play with several acts. Some of the characters who enter have short roles to play, others, much larger. Some are villains and others are good guys. But all of them are necessary, otherwise they wouldn't be in the play. Embrace them all, and move on to the next act." Mr. Dyer is saying that, sure, there are people and things that may hurt us and we may not like the end result, but forgive, let go, and move on, choosing to learn and turn the situation into a positive. People come into our lives for different reasons, and if we truly understand and know ourselves, we can turn anything around. All we have to do is forgive and move on. Personally, I had built up a massive amount of hate for WWE, and even though I had forgiven them numerous times for situations that hurt me, I couldn't move on and truly let that hate disappear as long as I stayed there. Eventually, I had to just let go and move on, and I've since forgiven everything. They do not make it easy by still trying to control and harass me through their attorneys, but I have forgiven them and have used that experience for motivation in all other areas of my life. I have had to accept that the past is over and done and will never change. It only existed in my mind, and I had zero control over any of it. I have had to remind myself to release myself of my past and look ahead to my new goals and aspirations. A great quote by Lao Tzu is, "Someone must risk returning injury with kindness, or hostility will never turn to goodwill."

Waking up with hate and resentment and going to bed the same way is the perfect recipe for disaster. It isn't always easy being the one who forgives, but once it has been done, a weight will be removed from your back and you will feel gratified and ecstatic. It is ok to be angry and have resentment, but we can't hold onto it forever unless we want that kind of internal pain. Whether it is a family member, a loved one, or just someone you don't like, let it go, forgive, and move on because the world is a much more enjoyable place when filled with love.

BEING AVERAGE ISN'T NECESSARILY
A BAD THING

Ok, so here I am writing a motivational book implementing many different techniques and strategies to improve our lives, and I have a part saying being average is ok? Yep, I said it! Not everyone has that drive for more. Some people do and I hope this book helps them find it, much like certain books did for me in my life. Others may just want to improve their lives in one area and this book can help them, too. Then there are those who are totally content being average. Who are any of us to judge how anyone lives their life? Happiness is a state of mind and success isn't something that magically makes happiness appear! If this is you and you are 100 percent happy and not hurting yourself or anyone else and life is good, who the hell is anyone to ridicule you?

But it goes the other way too. I was recently talking to a good friend of mine and he was telling me about a man in his 40s who used to wrestle. This guy is very bitter about the wrestling business, which really is no shocker, but he is your stereotypical "worker bee" type person. He likes being told what to do and when to do it. He watches the media and believes what he sees and hears, and he forms opinions on things without knowing the facts. He holds on to what other people have told him and has no desire to think for himself. This is 100 percent ok, but this particular person is very judgmental towards people who have a drive for success and for helping people. He made several comments about my leaving WWE, saying I should just be thankful and take whatever they offer me. He knew zero about the situation, he doesn't know me and my values and what I believe in, and he couldn't understand why someone would turn down all that money. I am ok with his "worker bee" mentality and don't take it personally, as he has never had a desire for more in life. So what I am saying is that it is ok if you have this type of personality where you enjoy being told what to do and if having the weekends off makes you happy to work for others during the rest of the week. But don't judge others because you don't understand their desire for more! Another great quote from Napoleon Hill says, "We refuse to believe that which we don't understand" and just because we don't understand something, doesn't mean we have the right to judge and hate.

Some of the happiest people I have ever met have been what others would consider overweight. There is a portion of the population that just don't give a damn what they look like and love food and are happy campers. I think that is totally great. Like I said, we are all different and all have different events and situations in our lives that helped shape our beliefs. So if you are what society says is overweight and you are happy, don't struggle to lose weight if it makes you miserable. I do think it is worth looking into why you have the feelings you do, as it may help unlock some deeper things going on, but if not, it is no hair off my back. Every single one of us is different and special in our own unique way and it is our choice how we want to live our lives. If eating pizza with friends and watching sporting events or lounging around on the weekends at the pool having drinks makes you the happiest, I say, hell yeah! and keep living your life! The most important thing, no matter who you are, is that you don't judge others. Just be you and be happy. The success-minded people have no right to judge the average-minded people and the average-minded people have no right to judge the success-minded people. Live, love, laugh. We can all coexist in peace if we keep this in mind.

THE POWER OF BEING HUNGRY

Mike Tyson will forever go down as one of the greatest heavyweight boxers of all time. There was a point where "The Baddest Man on the Planet" was undefeated in the world of boxing and at 23 years of age held the heavyweight boxing championship. Nobody could hang with Iron Mike in the ring and he had his eyes on Evander Holyfield, whom many thought would be Tyson's greatest challenge. First though, he had to fight a man by the name of Buster Douglas. He was a very good boxer, but not many boxing experts would rank him in Mike Tyson's league. At this point in Tyson's career, he was undefeated and had knocked out nearly all of his opponents. His confidence was sky-high and he had more money than he knew what to do with. He has gone on record to say that during this period, he was slacking in his training and partying all the time. It hadn't stopped him up until this point because he was an unbelievably talented human being and he believed he was as tough as the headlines said. I think it is safe to say Mike Tyson was still hungry at this point, but maybe not quite as much as when he had very little money and no real security.

His opponent, Buster Douglas, was not just another boxer going in the ring that night to get knocked out and collect his check. He was a man who was beyond hungry. He was determined and had that undeniable hunger that when engaged is nearly impossible to stop. Even a force like Tyson couldn't contain that power. You see, Buster Douglas' mother had passed away the month prior, and she had told her son before she passed that she believed he could beat Mike Tyson. On top of that, he had just separated from his wife, and the mother of his 11-year-old son was seriously ill. All of this created a hunger in Buster Douglas to go out there for one night and do the impossible. On that infamous night, he knocked out Iron Mike Tyson.

How many times have you heard amazing success stories about people who came from horrible childhoods and were able to turn it all around and become incredibly successful? It happens a lot more than you may think. People who come from a background of struggling know the value of hard work. Nothing was handed to them and they learned early on that in order to survive, they had to be hungrier than anyone around them. They also learned not to feel sorry for themselves and their beliefs matched their work ethic. I feel you have to experience bad to truly appreciate the good and people who struggle early on know what bad feels like. They have an insatiable hunger to fight, scratch, and claw their way into a better life.

Now this isn't the case for everyone who struggled early in life or comes from a less than ideal background. And you can still be successful without a rough childhood. I came from what you would call your average middle-class family, and I had a great childhood. I had very loving parents who made sure we had everything we needed to live a good life. I always had this fire inside me to work hard, but I never had to struggle early on so it was never a state of desperation. Fast-forward, though, to when I was 25 and out of wrestling, working in a BBQ joint. I was drinking a bottle of vodka a night, and I lived in a tiny studio apartment with a bed and a couch my ex-girlfriend let me borrow, with a flimsy TV stand and TV. Going through that life for a year—while working twelve-hour days, living day to day on the tips I was making—I figured out real fast what being hungry was about. Now it isn't the saddest story out there and is far from bad considering what many people have gone through, but it sent the correct message and I knew I never wanted to live like that ever again. From that point on, I would never get complacent. I take great pride in knowing that, no matter how much money I have been blessed with, my work ethic just keeps getting stronger and stronger. I work harder now than I ever have and I never plan on slowing down, as long as my health permits! The best way I can describe the power of being hungry is that it's like being held underwater. It is such a helpless feeling, and the panic makes you deplete oxygen at a rapid rate, causing your body to flail in every direction. It takes every ounce of energy for you to break free and that first gasp of air is the greatest feeling in the world! Being hungry for more feels a lot like that and when you feel it, you know, trust me on that.

I feel for competitive athletes and fighters. Knowing where your opponent came from and what they are currently experiencing in life can potentially help you. If you have a mixed martial arts fight approaching and you know your opponent is dealing with something, it may serve you to adjust your training and create a story in your own mind to match that hunger in your training. Had Mike Tyson known what Buster Douglas was going through, perhaps he would have trained a little bit differently. I'm not saying that it would have changed the outcome and that Buster Douglas still wouldn't have had the fight of his life, but it would have prepared him a hell of a lot better. It is amazing what a little storytelling can do for our work ethic if we have trouble creating that fire from within on a regular basis. Sometimes just making up a scenario in your head to get yourself fired up and hungry is all that is takes. Everyone is different in how they respond to things, though. Understanding the power of being hungry will help us when we need it most. I'm not telling anyone to starve, but if you want more, always stay hungry!

GROWTH MINDSET VS FIXED MINDSET

What is the difference between a growth mindset and a fixed mindset? The book that introduced me to this concept is *Mindset* by Carol Dweck. It is very informative and I highly recommend it to anyone wanting to better understand themselves and why they think the way they do. According to Dweck, people with a fixed mindset believe their basic qualities, like their intelligence or talent, are simply fixed traits. They spend the majority of their time documenting their intelligence or talent instead of developing them. They also believe that talent alone creates success, not effort. According to Dweck, they are wrong and I fully agree with her. In a growth mindset, people believe that their most basic abilities can be developed through dedication and hard work—brains and talent are just the starting point. This view creates a love of learning and a resilience that is essential for great accomplishment. Virtually all great people have had these qualities. I have always thrived on the growth mindset and truly believe nothing can replace hard work and dedication along with a positive mindset. I do believe we all have different starting points for talents and different confidence levels, which do greatly affect things. It has always made me wonder how people could just think they had no control over their lives. While there have been some successful people with a fixed mindset, they were just so beyond talented that it got them by for a long time. Ultimately, it will catch up to them. Here are several other signs of each mindset thanks to learngrowflourish.com:

FIXED MINDSET:

- Stay within their comfort zone and choose to attempt tasks that they know they can achieve so as not to fail in front of others

- Avoid new opportunities or tasks if they believe they may not do well

- Need to price their intelligence or talent
- Respond to mistakes as failures

GROWTH MINDSET:

- View new tasks as opportunities to learn
- Pick tasks that may challenge them rather than staying in their comfort zone
- Accept that mistakes might happen when they are trying new tasks

Keeping a positive mindset and setting goals go hand in hand with having a growth mindset. I often wonder if that is why the law of attraction has worked so well for me. I am a growth mindset individual and the two things feed so well off of each other. People who are negative more times than not seem to have a fixed mindset. One thing Dweck said that really resonates with me is that you need to have a passion for learning rather than a hunger for approval. I have seen this dramatically change in myself over the years and it has changed my life tremendously. I thrive on challenging myself and have learned that failure is totally ok. It is what you take from it and how you learn and apply it to the rest of your life that matters. Rather than being scared of failing, I am optimistic and excited to learn. After I walked away from WWE, not once did I say, "Oh my God, what if I fail and why am I doing this?" Instead, I am happy and beyond excited to be free and to challenge myself doing what I love in life. There is no haze influencing my vision anymore and the road ahead is wide open for me to drop the pedal to the metal and attack life!

A guy by the name of Phil Brooks, or CM Punk, as he's known in the UFC and WWE, also has what one would consider a growth mindset. I don't agree with everything he has said and done in the past, especially against me, but that doesn't change his mindset. He walked away from WWE years ago after being used in a main event role for quite some time. After leaving, he announced that he was going to fight for the UFC and was met with excitement from his hardcore followers and disbelief and resentment from a whole host of other people. You see, Punk had never had a mixed martial arts fight or really any true training outside of some jiujitsu. He was a full time WWE Superstar and that is where his time and effort went. But it was something he really wanted to do and he viewed the challenge as an opportunity to grow. Win, lose, or draw, he is truly challenging himself. That is why, despite our past, I have gone on record to offer my support and encouragement. He is exhibiting unlimited courage, and I am proud to see him challenge himself so deeply. I will say I feel he has put tremendous pressure on himself by accepting a fight with someone at the level of Mickey Gall, but you have to respect that he wants to challenge himself. If this truly is his full-time profession from here on out, then whatever happens in the fight will be used for motivation for his next fight. He may or may not do well as a fighter, but I commend him for going all in, and it will be interesting to witness either way.

If you think you fall into the fixed mindset group and you want to make changes, the first step is being aware of this. Be conscious of your thought patterns and how you view things to find things you want to change. If you are 100 percent happy in a fixed mindset and have no doubt that is who you are, and you never want to change, I totally respect that and say keep doing you. I personally feel having a growth mindset allows us more opportunities and a more fulfilled life over time, but everyone has to make their own choices.

Having a growth mindset in today's world isn't always easy. We must block out the world and choose to just go for it and to make ourselves happy no matter what anyone else thinks. The journey of life is about growing and evolving, and I have no doubt that if you can embrace and work on the traits of a growth mindset, you will grow and flourish in happiness.

UNLIMITED COURAGE

When I was a kid, I loved watching Care Bears with my sister. I thought it was cool how they could shoot their powers out of their stomachs! The one character that instantly caught my attention was Brave Heart. He exemplified unlimited courage and took control in times when others wanted to run. It is funny how something so simple can stick with you or resonate with you so strongly. I have always been drawn to courage and feel it is a must in order to achieve anything of great meaning. Courage has played a pivotal role in my life time and time again. Even at a young age, I would not tolerate what I perceived to be bullshit. I do not condone fighting, but sometimes you just have to shut someone up or teach someone with their own medicine. Growing up, if there was a kid in our neighborhood who was being problematic—bullying and stealing—I would take it into my own hands to go fight that kid and restore order in our awesome neighborhood. Looking back, was that the right thing to do? Probably not, but I have always had this courage inside of me and it has always worked well for me.

Another instance, which occurred in fifth grade, was when a kid who was known as someone who enjoyed fighting messed up my science project for no reason before the judging took place. I asked him why he would do that and when he responded by insulting me and showing no remorse, I took it into my own hands to show him what unlimited courage looks and feels like. That kid went to school with me for the rest of our school days and never looked at me or had a problem with anyone after that.

This chapter isn't about fighting, but about having that instinctual feeling to do right. The fact of the matter is that I had the courage to stand up for what I believed in at that time. Fear is a powerful emotion, but many of us miss out on moments of greatness by not taking advantage of the courage that lies inside of us. How many times have you felt absolutely horrible about yourself because you lacked the courage to do what you really wanted? How many beautiful women have you let slip on by because you lacked the courage to say hello and just take a chance? Likewise, ladies, how many times have you seen a man and wished he would come say hello because you lacked the courage to follow your intuition and say hello first?

Having unlimited courage comes with learning about yourself and loving yourself. It comes with believing in yourself and having an unwavering confidence. Through experiences in my life, I have learned to trust my instincts and never let something not work because I didn't have enough courage. Without unlimited courage, I do not believe I could have overcome my ankle injury in WWE. As a matter a fact, I 100 percent know I wouldn't have even existed as Ryback or in the WWE at all after my ankle injury had I not had the courage to stand up for myself and what was right. It took courage for me to come back and have the opportunity to live my dream. Fast-forward to right now and I am doing something not a lot of people involved in wrestling would have the courage to do as I speak about all of the problems within the organization. I have decided that I want to help make wrestling better, not just for the promoter, who is a billionaire, but for the men and women who dedicate their lives to the business of professional wrestling and are the core of the brand. I don't know if it will hurt my chances of ever going back, but I don't care. I am functioning at a level of no fear at this point in my life and unlimited courage rules my universe. We all have this power inside of us and it can be applied to any situation or circumstances that may arise. I promise you that once you can tap into your unlimited courage, it will forever change your life for the better!

YOU DICTATE WHO YOU ARE, NOT YOUR JOB

What we do to earn a living is only a part of us and doesn't tell the whole story of who we are. Who we are goes much deeper than how others see us or stereotype us. If someone chooses to be a janitor and cleans and picks up after others for a living, that isn't all that he is. That person could have a wife and kids and be extremely happy in life. He could be involved in his community and donate his time to charities. He could be comfortably well off or even wealthy, but perhaps just enjoys staying busy.

Many people think celebrities or famous athletes are the same in real life as they are on TV. It always amazes me when wrestling fans act shocked when I act like a normal person or do something funny. Early on in my WWE career, I played a character that pretty much just screamed, "Feed me more" and was an ultra-aggressive ass kicker in the ring. Many fans just assumed that was my personality 24/7, even though you would never assume that about an actor you saw in a movie. Who we are as individual human beings goes so deep that a job isn't much in the grand scheme of things. We are emotional beings, and I enjoy being in touch with every single emotion I can. I never want to be one dimensional or limited, and nobody else should either. I am the same person today that I was before I was on TV or when I was working as a server at Smokey Bones. I have learned and evolved in that time, but I am still the same human being at my core as I always have been.

People let their jobs dictate their self-esteem, which is a mistake that will leave you unfulfilled and empty. Our jobs only dictate a part of our financial situation and they don't define us. They don't dictate our happiness. What we do to make money in this life isn't who we ultimately are. That lies inside of us.

I CAN > I CAN'T

I can't tell you how much *I can* has helped me in my life. I can tell you *I can't* has never and will never help me in life. Ever since I was a kid, I have loved challenging myself and even if I did something that I wasn't good at right away, I have tried not to say I can't. An I-can mindset drives me to want to get better rather than saying I can't and giving up. I look back and smile when I see the things I did growing up to improve my abilities, things most people wouldn't think about working at. Because of my confidence and I-can attitude, I found it fun and pleasurable to see my progress. For instance, I loved playing baseball growing up. I would pitch from time to time, but it was never my main thing. I remember having a bad game when fairly young and instead of getting discouraged, I went into our backyard and threw ball after ball against a wall, working on all my pitches. For a guy who never really had the desire to be a pitcher, I did extremely well when I did pitch by having the I-can attitude. Another instance was in high school during football season. As a young kid, I was always the fastest kid in the neighborhood and as fast as anyone in school, but at the high school level, there were some really fast guys. I would come home and work on my sprints at night to build my explosiveness and conditioning.

We are all going to come across challenges and situations where we don't excel, but we can be our best if we think *I can*. I'm not talking about lying to ourselves here and just saying, "I can" and leaving it at that. Quite frankly, that won't get you very far. It is ok to understand that you didn't perform well, but then you have to take steps to do better next time. Unless you've been born with a physical disability or have suffered an injury that prevents you from doing something, you are fully capable. The thing that separates us is our mindset. Even people with disabilities show us unbelievable feats every day. They take those disabilities and turn them into positives because they believe *I can* to the fullest. I still remember my first main event pay-per-view match and being so excited before going out there. I was pacing, as I had so much energy I couldn't stand still. I kept affirming to myself I can do this, I can do this, I can do this. The phrase is simply empowering and when said with conviction and full belief can fuel the human mind and body to great things. People who get caught up in *I can't* sell themselves short every time and miss out on experiencing some great moments in life. The great thing is that you can instantly change the I-can't mindset to an I-can mindset at any moment. It just takes one second to forever change that, and I promise when you do, you will never regret it. Every day we wake up, we have a chance to say, "I can" and apply it to anything we want. I encourage you to embrace the power of *I can* and see what positive changes it can help bring to your life.

DEATH

I have not experienced a lot of death in my lifetime, and I am very thankful to have my family and friends all around me. It is the true unknown with life, and many of us try not to think about it and take life for granted. As a WWE wrestler, I used to visit sick children who were not going to live for very much longer. Going into those hospital rooms and seeing the families and getting a small glimpse into what they were going through was one of the hardest things I have ever had to do. The kids were always in such great spirits and so happy in the moment, but knowing what they'd gone through (some had had as many as 75 surgeries before the age of 11) really fucking rocks you at your core. It makes you ashamed when you leave and worry about your problems, knowing there are so many great human beings out there who are suffering and going through things none of us even want to imagine. I choose to believe that once we die, our soul (or energy or whatever you choose to call it) moves on to the next part of life. We can sit here all day long and try to convince ourselves of what that is, but I just choose to believe that it will be amazing. Even so, the fear of death is something we all have dealt with. I love life so much and I don't want to think about dying, but I have accepted it and realize my time will come. The best thing we can do is accept it and choose to feel good about it, hoping to go in a peaceful, harmonious way.

Many of us worry about our family, animals, and friends living and dealing with our loss if we were to move on. The one thing I neglected for so long was doing a will and making sure my family is taken care of if anything were to happen. I have since invested in a life insurance policy, as well, because I feel it is selfish not to leave something behind for those around you when you die. It isn't something I want to dwell on, but better safe than sorry.

A hard thing for me to accept is my dogs being without me. I love them more than anything, and dogs in general are the most loving creatures on our planet. The thought of Sophie, Sonny, Secret, and Shera not knowing where I am truly saddens me. Obviously, I don't sit around thinking about this all the time, but when I hear of death, it is things like this that go through my mind. The best we can do no matter what thoughts we have on death is to think good and loving thoughts about the situation. If you worry like me, make sure to communicate with someone about taking care of your loved ones if sudden death were to occur.

As I sit and write this, I'm seated on an airplane, as I frequently am. While I know airplanes are safe, it still is something I think about. There is something about not having any control that can be horrifying for many people, including myself. I have had to learn to just think good thoughts and trust the process, as my job quite simply requires me to travel constantly. I always say thank you to God/the Universe for this safe flight from here to there, and upon landing say thank you for this safe landing. If the pilot is standing outside the cockpit upon exiting, I always say thank you, as pilots have as much responsibility as anyone on our planet.

As I mentioned earlier, I haven't experience a lot of death in my life. My mother's father passed away when I was just a baby. I did meet him once and it makes me happy my mother got to share me with him for a little while, as I'm sure he was very proud. My grandparents on my father's side have both passed on, as well. My grandfather passed when I was younger, and that was the only funeral I have ever been to. It was a surreal experience seeing a lifeless body up close, but it wasn't terrifying to me. My grandmother passed while I was on the road full time, and I missed the funeral. I have missed quite a few big things I shouldn't have missed because I put my job first, and that is something I won't ever do again. We used to take family vacations to California to see them as kids. While their passing saddened me greatly, I had not seen them much over the years. I felt sad for my dad and uncle more than anything, as those were their parents.

We all handle death differently and it is something none of us truly has an answer to. When I lose a pet, I have found that finding another dog to love has helped me more than anything, even though you can never truly replace a pet you've loved. When Roxy passed away at twelve years old, it was so tough on me. She had slowed down in her old age but appeared in great health. When I first moved home before returning on the road as Ryback, I would spend the night at my father's house every Wednesday, as I was living in an apartment down the road and couldn't bring the dogs over there. I would hang out with them all night, just so I could be around them a bit before leaving on the road again for five days. One week while on the road, my dad called me and told me Roxy was very sick and not eating well, but that he was keeping an eye on her. I got home on a Wednesday and went over there to see the dogs and spend the night, and Roxy was on the floor not moving. My father was at work, and it was the most terrifying thing to see. She was alive, but her stomach was so swollen. I just knew it wasn't good, but it was nighttime and the vet was closed. She got up and started showing more life, which gave me some comfort, but something just told me this was it. I put her in my bed and slept with her and Shera, and Roxy cuddled up against me all night. When I woke up, her stomach was even more distended and I broke down holding her in my arms, just telling her how much I loved her. We brought her to the vet and they delivered the bad news of a tumor, most likely cancerous, rupturing inside her and causing internal bleeding. There was an operation they could attempt, but at her age, they didn't think it was worth the pain and suffering for her. Roxy was totally at peace, and I could tell just looking at her, she was ready to go. The loving, once-feisty pit bull who used to play relentlessly told me all I needed to be told with her eyes. My dad and I held her as they put her down. It was the hardest thing to do, but being able to love her in her final moments and see her pass pain-free gave me the closure I never had with Pebbles and Bam Bam. I had paintings of Roxy done by a professional artist for both my dad's house and mine, along with a collage of pictures of Roxy over the years, so her memory will always live on. When I got home, my concern shifted to my dog Shera, who lives at my father's house. She had been around Roxy for almost eight years and now was all alone. She was beyond sad, and that hurt just as badly as having to put Roxy down. About two weeks passed and my dad told me his neighbors had a pit bull and French bulldog mix that they always left outside in the heat. Their backyard was all dirt and filled with junk and debris. When I looked over my dad's wall to see if she was out there, the cutest little dog came crawling out of a pile of junk, where she hid for the shade in the 110-degree weather. Right then and there, I knew this dog was mine and I was going to get her out of that miserable life she was living. I went around and let her out of the side gate, and she was the most adorable dog I had ever seen. I put her back in her yard and went and knocked on the neighbor's door. Nobody answered, so I went home and wrote a note explaining our situation with Roxy and that we would like to give their dog a loving home with a friend. I also included who I was, just in case they were wrestling fans, hoping it would help my chances of getting her. Luckily, they were, so all it took was a couple 8x10s and saying hello, and they gave her to me on the spot! I named her Secret, and she and Shera became the best of friends. I could never replace Roxy, but I could give a new love to a new dog, and it greatly helped with the grieving process. That is my experience with death, and I hope in some way it can help if you are going through the loss of a loved one.

EXCUSES

When things don't go the way we'd hoped, we can come up with many different excuses. Ultimately, the best way to move past it is to accept blame for it and believe in your ability to get the result you want next time. Or just totally accept it and move on to bigger and better things. Excuses will just hold us back in life and prevent us from evolving if we let them take over. We have all made excuses, and it's natural to want to turn to them in the judgmental world we live in, but we have to block that out and just accept things at times. We mainly make excuses for the following reasons:

- Fear of failure
- Fear of embarrassment
- Fear of uncertainty
- Fear of change
- Fear of making mistakes
- Fear of responsibility
- Fear of success
- Lack of confidence

Fear plays a major role in us making excuses, as you can see. Typically, the fear of these things will result in a lack of confidence, as well. It all comes back to self-development, knowing who we are, and making changes where we see fit. It is ok if you have made excuses before—we all have! You just need to step back and realize why you made the excuse and learn and move on. It's also ok to realize why we failed at something and to work on fixing those reasons. That is entirely different from making excuses. For example, if I wanted to bench press 550 pounds and I attempted it and failed to lift the weight all the way back up, I could say, well, I didn't get it because my shoulder hurt and my form was off.

But rather than just telling people I couldn't do it because my shoulder was hurt, I could work on my form and do the things necessary to correct my shoulder pain, so that when I attempt it again, I have a better shot of making the lift. Like I have said before, it is totally ok to fail and we all are going to fail many times in our lives if we actually live life and take chances. It is ok, and we don't need excuses. We just need reasons and motivation to improve ourselves one day at a time. Fail, learn, and try again—and save the excuses!

TREAT OTHERS WITH LOVE

There is so much hate and separation in our world, and it is unfortunate. There are billions of people, and while we are all very different, we are also all one and the same. We are all made up of the same stuff—bones, blood, and everything in between. The only thing that is different between us is what we are surrounded with and what ideas enter our minds.

There is so much stress in our world that we all seem to be very judgmental and filled with anger towards others, usually for no reason. Far too many pry into other people's lives, to criticize and judge and hate, when all we should be concerned with is ourselves and our loved ones. Social media is a big part of this problem, and I will discuss this further in the social media section below. We have to take the steps necessary to love others more. We need to love ourselves, first and foremost. We cannot truly give love if we don't have love for ourselves. Once we love ourselves and learn to live without judgment, life takes on a whole new meaning.

Something that always hurt me when wrestling in the WWE was the way certain so-called fans would act. I remember many nights in 2012 and 2013 where I would be one of the last ones to leave the building, and there would be hundreds of fans waiting outside. Many nights, even with a long drive ahead of me, I would stop and sign autographs and take pictures, sometimes for 30 to 40 minutes, to try and make everyone happy. I was in the main event and wanted fans to feel good when they left that night. But no matter what I did, it never was enough for some fans. I would have people screaming profanities because they wanted two autographs instead of one, or their picture was blurry, or any other excuse you can think of. There were some nights where it was already 11 o'clock, and I had a 5-hour drive ahead of me and hundreds of fans. I would let the fans know I had a long drive and apologize for not sticking around to take pics or sign autographs. I would shake all the fans' hands and try to be as friendly as possible. It would really hurt when I would see negative tweets saying I was a piece of shit for not doing pictures or autographs, and to this day it truly bothers me we have people out there that are that selfish and ignorant. It slowly turned me away from some fans, as there was no way to distinguish who would end up saying stuff like that later on. I would remind myself daily to treat all people with love. If anyone approached me at a time where I was busy or if I felt they were rude in how they addressed me, I would simply say, "No, thank you" and leave it at that. There are many times when I am in a public gym with my headphones on, listening to my Holosync meditation. It is 60–90 minutes long and I do not like to take the headphones off or break my focus for that period. There have been many times people have come up in the gym and I just say, "No, thank you, when I am all done, please." I have seen a few people get very offended by this and go on to leave very nasty comments on my social media pages, and that hurts. These people approach with a sense of entitlement and nothing but yes is acceptable. For me, doing the things necessary to keep me happy and mentally healthy, so I can continue to perform daily at a high level, comes first. It is important for us to be able to see both sides of the fence and to try to be more compassionate and loving in general. There are far more important things in life than posting hourly updates and pictures of yourself with other people on social media. If we would not be so quick to judge, even when we don't get something we want, ultimately the world would be a better place.

Another thing that hurts me is when I see people who are rude to people like waiters or someone they perceive to be under them. I have gone out to eat with other people and seen them act like complete assholes to the server for no reason. I have had to ask them to knock it off, and I would apologize to the server because that type of behavior is never warranted. That person serving is a human being and they are just living their life to the best of their ability. The jobs we have do not make us better than other people. Every human being on this planet serves a role, regardless of how small.

It isn't always easy to show love for all people, because there are a lot of bad people in the world. The best thing we can do is think a positive thought to them and move on. I have begun doing this with people who attack me on social media. I simply wish them the best, block them, and move on. It makes me feel better about the situation, and that is all I can do. Just try understanding we are all humans, and we come from one universe, or whatever you want to say. We are one and giving hate to others ultimately makes us attract hate within ourselves.

Section 3

SELF-IMPROVEMENT

SOCIAL MEDIA

Where do I begin with this? So many great things can be achieved with social media and things like Twitter (@Ryback22), Instagram (@TheBigGuyRyback22), Facebook, Tumblr (TheBigGuyRyback22), Snapchat (Ryback247), and my bread and butter, FeedMeMore.com. They allow us to stay in contact with family and friends that we might have otherwise lost contact with. We can promote good causes and raise awareness in a way never before possible, and social media has created new jobs and opportunities for entrepreneurs to live their dreams. It can bring us endless hours of entertainment, helping us to forget about the seriousness of the real world and just let loose and laugh. It can give us inside looks into the lives of people we watch on TV and interact with them unlike any other time before. We can find lost pets quicker than ever and help catch criminals, making videos or pictures go viral. There truly is a plethora of good that comes from social media, but sadly, where there is good, there is also bad.

Somewhere along the way, this amazing technology opened the floodgates for a certain group of individuals, which seems to grow by the day, to use social media in a negative fashion. In the real world, we can, for the most part, control whom we surround ourselves with. And I strongly believe that we are whom we spend time with. Rarely would you see goal-driven, smart, family-oriented individuals surrounding themselves with people who aren't like-minded. This isn't to say you won't have friends who are very different than you, but typically we enjoy being around people who share similar interests as us and don't bring us down or insult us. Social media allows these negative individuals access to our worlds. People whom we would never give the time of day to or want anywhere near our friends and families now can reach out and say things to us we couldn't even fathom someone saying. These people are truly lost and have no sense of direction or purpose, and they try to bring down everyone around them. They say things they'd never say if they saw you in person, hiding behind their walls of insecurities inside their houses, feeling untouchable.

Human beings have no right to judge other human beings, yet so many of us do it without hesitation. If this applies to you, consider that nothing is accomplished from this sort of behavior, and you waste valuable time pushing negative energy onto others. Rather than wishing illness, accidents, and death on people you don't like, focus on bettering yourself. Social media brings out the worst in humans, and it is so upsetting seeing full-grown adults who speak of how much they love God and Jesus and their families saying the worst things you could imagine. It is gut wrenching to see that these people hold normal jobs and are part of society with a family and kids. I have had people approach me at airports looking to get wrestling merchandise signed to sell on eBay and when I've said, "No, thank you," they've posted on social media wishing plane crashes and death on me and my family. Humans were not designed to act this way, and it is time for this behavior to stop altogether, and it starts with each and every one of us.

Luckily, social media technology allows us to block these people from our accounts. Sadly, we sometimes have to read their utter bullshit first, but at least it ends there and we can move on. I have made the decision to use social media, as I find it important to keep my finger on the pulse of things as I build my brand and business, but I take breaks from reading comments as it is beyond frustrating reading some of the things people say. It truly isn't worth my time. I know who I am as a man and a human being and don't need the opinions of people who don't truly know me, though I do appreciate the support and love I get as well. I designate certain periods of time to go on and eliminate the negativity and then forget it. Give it a try. It is a much better use of your free time if you don't check it multiple times a day.

Another problem with social media is that a lot of us allow it to consume our lives. For example, you'll see a family out to dinner and they are all on their phones before they even look at the menus. Or people at the gym on their phones even while working out. I have been guilty of this in the past, always having my phone on me or by me. It takes away from truly living life in real life. If I didn't think social media was so valuable for certain aspects of my life and brand and what I am trying to achieve at a world level, I would have deleted all of it years ago! I have gotten in the habit of going periods of time where I don't use my phone outside of calls or texts with family or friends. I always try to read for 20–30 minutes a day and listen to audio books for 2–3 hours a day when driving. If I am eating with a friend, I set my phone down out of sight and I don't check it. It is too easy to let technology consume us, so be conscious of it and do your best. I think it is paramount for parents to educate their kids on proper use of and behavior on social media and the potential risks of saying things online that they would otherwise never say. We live in an amazing universe and technology is developing at a rapid pace. It is better to understand it and use it for good and not evil!

RIGHT AND WRONG

One of the most influential books for me years ago was a book called *Conversations with God* by Neale Donald Walsch. In this wonderful book, which I highly recommend to everyone, he says that there is no right or wrong, only what we believe. This is similar to a quote by Henry Ford, who said, "Whether you think you can, or you think you can't—you're right." My purpose for writing this part of the book isn't to challenge religion or anyone's beliefs but to raise awareness of what we know and how we came to know these things, which are embedded deep in our brains. The fact is that most of what we know or believe was taught to us by our parents or those who raised us.

We grow up believing our parents know it all. We just assume that what they teach us is best for us, but that isn't always the case. Most of what our parents know is from what they were taught growing up and most of what their parents knew was from what they were taught growing up and so on and so on. We all come from vastly different backgrounds. Some people come from rich families, some from middle class families, and some from poor families. If you look around the world, the differences are even more extreme, such as places like India where you see families naked for the most part living in the worst of conditions. Some people come from families that teach them good manners and morals and then you have people who have no concept of who and what they are or what life is about. They are content living off of other people and they have six kids. My point isn't to bash these people because that isn't what this is about. My point is to raise awareness on how we think and that we actually have a choice! There are many different types of people on this earth, good and bad, which leads to kids being brought up many different ways, but I firmly feel that no matter what our circumstances, we have the ability to evolve as we go through life. We may not be able to control who raised us or what they put into our minds, but we can control what we put in our minds *now* and this is very empowering. What we need to survive and to thrive and succeed in this world isn't just going to be given to us or taught to us. We have to wake up every day wanting to learn and better ourselves, which will ultimately better the world and those around us. There is unlimited knowledge in our world and we have to have that inner hunger to figure it out and apply it to our lives.

We must think for ourselves but, in order to do that, we must educate ourselves in the correct fashion. We can't just rely on the media to tell us what to think or trust newspapers to give us the facts because the majority of it is absolute garbage. Don't be afraid to think for yourself and form your own conclusions because doing so is a major step in finding out who you really are. We have control over our lives. Unexpected things can and probably will occur, but we have a choice how we react. Inside each and every one of us is an all-powerful force. It is just up to us to find it!

SETTING GOALS

I cannot stress enough the importance of setting goals and the powerful impact they can have on your life. At the very least, you will wake up with purpose and know why you are doing the things you do. To quote Rhonda Byrnes, author of *The Secret*:

"Your power is in your thoughts, so stay awake. In other words, remember to remember."

The power of setting goals simply is that they help us to remember what we want. I always heard as a kid about setting goals, but it didn't sink in until much later in life. As a kid I excelled in pretty much anything I did so what did I need goals for? Looking back, I can only imagine what I could have accomplished had I focused and really strived for some big things. One of my favorite methods of goal setting is to use visualization boards, something I learned about from *The Secret*.

Using visualization boards is essentially about writing down your goals, so I bought a dry erase board and hung it up in my bedroom and mapped out some things I wanted to happen in my life. Today I have these boards stationed in strategic places in my house, and I have many different types of "goal boards," as I like to call them. I have a board for my goals for the year, where I map out a number of things I am striving for in that particular year. If there is something I don't achieve in that year, I move it to the next year until I eventually get it. I have my Life Goal board, which has what I want to accomplish on a grand scale by the time my life is over. These are some pretty amazing large dreams and it is cool to read it each week to remind myself of the big picture. I have another board for why I live my life and wake up each and every day. This is something I got from Tony Robbins, and I think it is an incredible concept that can help you hop out of bed excited and ready to live life. It will enhance your life over time when you see what you want staring back at you in your own home. I also have goal boards for possessions, as I find it very fun and satisfying to work hard and be able to reward myself at times. I am a big believer in saving for the future and planning ahead, but I also believe we have to live life in the moment and treat ourselves. I want to enjoy the greatest things in my life now as well as the future. I often see people who pinch pennies and save save save at the expense of enjoying life today, and I have a feeling that when they are older they will be doing the same thing. Eventually, life will pass them by and all that saving will have created a life of fear. I'm not saying go out and blow your savings. I'm just saying don't be afraid to live a little today. These possession goal boards are some of the most fun ones for me as it is cool to see what you can come up with and actually get.

I used to try and do this in my head, but I found that when I started writing things down they started happening for me. When we see our goals each and every day, I believe on a subconscious level we start to adapt and change our behavior so we can reach these goals. Oftentimes, I won't even notice I have made changes in my life that are helping me get to my goals, and it amazes me every time. So go get a dry erase board or you can check out my Feed Me More Goal Boards at FeedMeMore.com. I know the impact vision boards have had on me and this is my way of making it easier for you. Start writing your wants and desires down and get the most out of life! I feel so strongly about this that if there is just one thing I could tell you to take from this book, this part on goals is it. Always remember what the great Prentice Mulford said: "Every thought of yours is a real thing—a force."

TIME MANAGEMENT

Author and speaker John C. Maxwell says, "Time management is an oxymoron. Time is beyond our control, and the clock keeps ticking regardless of how we lead our lives. Priority management is the answer to maximizing the time we have." Some people feel they have too much time on their hands, and they are constantly bored and don't know what to do with themselves. To them I say, prioritize what you want first. Figure out who you are and what you want and then you can figure out how to better manage your time. For many of us, though, there never seems to be enough time in the day to do everything we want. This chapter is directed at those who wish there was more time.

There are 24 hours in every day, but our perception of time changes. How we feel and how we approach our day can influence how quickly or slowly time goes for us. The first thing that I have found that helps is keeping a clean home and workplace. When things are cluttered and messy or there are a bunch of uncompleted tasks around the home, it can give you an overwhelming feeling of not having enough time. So get your house or workplace caught up first. Next, focus on the most important things in your life at the given time. If family and work are most important, then set aside the appropriate amount of time so that these two things are taken care of. If you are doing other things that are less important and your family and work life are suffering, take a step back and figure out what you need to do to take care of these things. Writing things down works wonders. When you can see something in front of you, it embeds it in your mind, and your actions follow.

Setting aside time for yourself is also extremely important. If you aren't happy and taking care of yourself, it is very hard for you to be of maximum service for others. Whether it be setting aside 30 minutes for physical activity or 15–20 minutes of meditation or watching an episode of your favorite TV show, taking just a little bit of time to take care of yourself will go a long way in helping you accomplish everything you need to.

Eliminating negative people, places, and things from your life is something you must do if you want to effectively manage your time. For example, social media, as great as it is for certain things, consumes far too much of our days. Set limits on your social media usage if you are always behind on things. Trust me, it isn't going anywhere, and you don't have to check it a hundred times a day. If we are neglecting the important things in our lives, eliminating the less important stuff is a must.

Getting adequate sleep so you wake up feeling energized and refreshed is so important. My section on waking up can help with your attitude on sleep and understanding it better. If you are getting less than satisfactory sleep, you are already at a huge disadvantage when you start your day. When we feel tired, the easiest of tasks can seem impossible. One thing that helped me on nights I was having trouble getting to sleep is a program called Holosync Sleep Suite from a man named Bill Harris, one of the people featured in the book *The Secret*. You can find out more at his website, www.centerpointe.com. Learning and applying different techniques such as this to our lives gives us a better chance to succeed. Don't let inadequate sleep be the reason you don't manage your time effectively.

FOCUS

To achieve maximum focus we need to eliminate distractions. Even as I sit and write right now, I have a meditation soundtrack and headphones on to tune out outside noise, and it helps me to really laser in on this. Albeit, I have two dogs lying on my lap on the couch, and I'm taking breaks to play with their ears and bellies. Anything can be a distraction, but one of the most common is cell phones, with their text messages and phone calls and easy access to apps like Twitter, Instagram, and Facebook. Family, kids, and pets also play a big part in distracting us. For me, hunger is totally distracting, so I always have to make sure I'm fed before I can really focus on something. (I ate a huge mahimahi and a tuna filet before sitting down to write this chapter.) For people with jobs where they are required to check and reply to emails, that can be a huge distraction when trying to focus in on a project. If you work from home, maybe it is the television. No matter what it is, they prevent us from focusing on the task at hand, and what should take 30 minutes might take an hour!

I use what I like to call Time Task Tubes (TTT) to help me focus in. This involves setting aside anywhere from 30 to 90 minutes where you do nothing except focus on the task at hand. If that means shutting your phone off or leaving it in another room, then so be it. Maybe you'll put on headphones and listen to some classical music while you concentrate or ask your family for some privacy while you do what you have to do. When you set aside a block of time for the TTT, there is no room for anything else! For instance, I'm learning Spanish right now, something I've always wanted to do. Each day I set aside a Time Task Tube of 30-90 minutes, depending on the day at hand, and I chip away at it. It is just me, the time, and the Spanish during this period. If I am studying a wrestling match, I don't use my phone during the match so I can totally take everything in. In today's world, those who can block out the distractions best are the ones I feel will be the most successful people. When your TTT time is up, give yourself a break and check your cell phone or emails. Set aside five minutes to focus on anything you want as long as you get back to your tasks afterwards. While it may seem like that is distracting you, giving yourself a reward for staying focused actually improves your focus.

Going hand in hand with focus is time management, which includes writing things down and planning ahead. Whether you do it daily, weekly, or monthly, using the notes section in your phone or writing out your tasks prior to doing them can help you tremendously in focusing. You can start the day with easier tasks to build some momentum or tackle the harder, more complex things first, whichever you prefer. The key is being prepared ahead of time so that you can maximize your days and nights. The great thing about being focused is that we get things done more quickly and then we can use that free time however we choose afterwards.

Staying focused on the present is the final thing I want to elaborate on. We cannot live in the past, whether good or bad, because it can hold us back from doing what we need to do today to make tomorrow better for ourselves. It is easier said than done, but it is imperative that we live by this. Maybe you went to an MMA class and got tapped out and felt embarrassed. So what? Show back up and keep showing up until you get so good you are the one tapping everyone out. Or maybe you took an acting class and fumbled over your words and everyone laughed at you. So what? Laugh at yourself and stay focused on your homework and don't fumble them the next time. Maybe you studied for a test and didn't get the grade you wanted. Learn from it and study harder and do better on the next one! Be thankful for the past, but don't let it hold you back from focusing to the best of your ability today.

VISUALIZATION

There is a saying that goes, "See it, feel it, believe it" and visualization is the "seeing it" part. This is such a powerful tool for mentally envisioning what you physically want out of life. When you are able to picture in your mind exactly what it is you want, whether it be scoring the winning touchdown or driving your dream car, it helps you to get closer to that dream becoming a reality. Napoleon Hill, whom I have mentioned had a great influence on me with his books, says, "Whatever the mind can conceive and believe, it can achieve." When I am envisioning something, I like to close my eyes and replay the scenario I am seeking out numerous times. I try to remain as focused as I can on this process and imagine how I would feel during the moment. There are times when I have some very big goals and it takes me a while to really get into the moment and believe that I could make this happen. These are the moments when I really need to focus and truly believe I am capable of anything I want to do. I will replay it over and over until I feel good about the situation. Things don't always work out how we envision them, and it is up to us to continue to visualize. Sometimes things take time and even though we may want something so badly right away, the timing just isn't right yet. The key is to be persistent and to stay hungry for that vision and to continue to see it. There are two visions that I have not yet been able to manifest, even though I believe and feel them very strongly each and every time. One is a match with Brock Lesnar from the UFC/WWE. It has been on its own vision board for three years now and I can truly see it and feel it being the greatest matchup of all time. Another major goal of mine, which has been on my vision board for five years, is becoming the WWE World Heavyweight Champion. The problem with these two visions is that I have zero control over the final decision to make these goals a reality. At least this was true when I was in the WWE. Now that I have left, I feel I have more power than ever to do the things I need to do to be happy and to gain control over making these visions a reality. I just am taking a different road to get to the final destination. If you truly want something, NEVER stop envisioning it! I assure you that practicing visualization will add to your life, so try it and get as good at it as you can!

HARD WORK ALWAYS WORKS

Hard work is why I have everything that I do in my life. I have always applied myself to things I take an interest in and it never has done me wrong. I mentioned a quote earlier in the book that has helped me tremendously that essentially says it isn't the hours you put in, but what you put into the hours. It is working hard, but being able to really focus on that work to get the most out of it. If you look at anybody who is anybody in any given field, more often than not they have worked very hard at what they do. The one question I often get is, "How do I know if I am working hard enough?" Well, you can see what others in your field are doing and gauge your actions on that. Secondly, you should have an internal sense of well-being if you are working to the best of your ability in the things that matter most for your goals. It is always smart to try to look at what you are doing from an outside perspective at times and make adjustments to your goals, as your internal threshold rises with the work that you do. What got you great results six months ago may need to be altered slightly for you to continue making progress for your goals and lifestyle.

I can tell you from experience that results don't always follow immediately. But if you are truly doing everything in your power to achieve your goals and you know deep down you are working as hard or harder than anyone else around you, and the results aren't coming, it may be time to reassess things. One thing to assess is whether you are happy. If the things you are doing don't make you happy or the work you do doesn't fulfill you, you need to get out and find something that does. I'm not saying you should quit your job and put yourself and your family in financial jeopardy. But perhaps start looking at other things that you could put your passion and hard work behind to get better results. At the very least, find a new hobby that you are passionate about to increase your happiness outside of work. There is nothing worse than killing yourself for other people's benefit and not being appreciated or rewarded when others apply half the effort and are hand-fed opportunity after opportunity. Control your destiny and set yourself up for other opportunities by planning ahead, then reap the rewards of your hard work.

Ultimately, hard work always works. Even if it doesn't ultimately pay off financially or the results are delayed, it will carry over into other aspects of your life. Keep finding ways to push yourself—mentally, physically, or spiritually—and your life will improve. A very good friend who is a successful bodybuilder out of Las Vegas told me when I was nineteen years old that everything works and nothing works, but one way or another, you got to put in the work! I have always held this quote close to me and it has never done me wrong. So what are you waiting for? Put the pedal to the metal and get the most out of your life!

FOCUSING ON ONE THING

I love to be good at everything I do. I understand I am not, but that doesn't take away the drive to be great at everything I have my hands on. For years and years, my job has been as a professional wrestler and I've had to live, eat, breathe, and sleep wrestling to get to the level I have. The drive for me to be my absolute best will never leave me and, to this day, I still watch one or two matches a day. Over the course of a year that is a lot of matches, on top of performing four to five nights a week and watching matches at our shows. In addition to wrestling, I love learning about new things and reading and listening to audio books. I love working out and boxing and jiujitsu. I want to shoot guns and eat out at places I have never been. It was getting to the point where I was stressing out about not having enough time to do the things I wanted to do. I was only home for a day or two a week and some of that was spent unpacking, packing, and doing laundry to go back on the road. I was trying to do too much with not enough time while also trying to relax from the relentless road schedule that is my life.

I came across a book called *The One Thing* by Jay Papasan and it totally opened my eyes to something that has always been a problem for me. I was spreading myself thin and not focusing enough on just one thing. This book taught me to narrow down how much I try to get done and pick one or two things I want to do while home. For example, I could just do boxing for a period of time and concentrate on that, rather than trying to cram in that and jiujitsu. Then when I am comfortable with where I am at boxing, I can focus on the jiujitsu. Or I could do one for a week and the other the next. Papasan proclaims that it takes focusing on one thing three to four hours a day in order to eventually become a master at it. I wholeheartedly agree and highly recommend the book to anyone trying to figure out what that one thing is for them.

I would sometimes try listening to several books in the same period, and I found this to be overwhelming even before coming across Jay's book. I learned to focus on one book at a time, which made learning from that one book much easier. It also feels good to finish books at a faster rate. You may enjoy doing a lot of things, which is totally fine if that is what makes you happy. But if you are trying to master something and are having difficulty focusing, this may be just what the doctor ordered!

MY RULES FOR SUCCESS

All of my life I have done things a little differently. I have lived a very successful life thus far, even though it has been far from perfect. I have always been able to accomplish anything I set my mind to and that isn't just luck. It is the mindset I use when I approach things. I truly believe greatness lies inside all of us and it is up to us to discover that greatness and live our lives to the best of our abilities and according to our own life values. The following rules are what have allowed me to be me and to continue to grow, take chances, and add value to my life.

1. Believe in Yourself – If you lack confidence in yourself and you don't trust yourself, then you are going to have an incredibly difficult time accomplishing what you want in your life. You have to believe in your abilities and in your mind even if everyone else doubts you. If you doubt yourself then that will become your reality. If you are lacking in confidence, find ways to boost it and raise your self-esteem. Believing in yourself is the fuel that runs the machine. Don't ever fail because there wasn't enough fuel in the tank!

2. Set Goals – We hear this time and time again, don't we? Yet somehow, it seems to be one of the most difficult things for people to follow through on. Is it because a lot of us are afraid of failing? Is it because we are too lazy? Do some of us just not know what we want? All of the above can be true, along with a host of other excuses. We can't expect greatness if we don't know what we want to be great at! Now, I don't think we need to map our days and nights out A-Z, but we have to know what the hell we want. We don't need to set ten plus goals a year (like I always do because I have always been a little obsessive), but setting one or two goals and attacking them on a daily basis will no doubt improve your life. Every year I set goals and if there are some I don't quite reach that year, then I move them to the top of the following year's goals.

Even if we don't quite get what we pictured in our heads, goals allow us to stay on track.

3. Work Hard and Spend Yourself – Whatever it is you choose to set your sights on, look at what the best people in that field are doing and find ways to either mimic that work ethic or to work even harder than them. I truly believe hard work always works and it is what separates good from great and great from legendary. The universe rewards hard work and effort and while things may not always come when we want them, ultimately they come when we need them most. Don't ever let someone else get what you want because they worked harder than you.

4. Educate Yourself – It isn't up to anyone in this world to make sure you understand life or learn about the things you need to learn. Sure, our parents teach us stuff when we are kids, but once we are old enough to think for ourselves, it is solely on us to learn. I never really understood money and I could have bitched and moaned that my parents should have taught me or the school system should have taught me and maybe they should have. But that isn't going to get me the skills and knowledge I need. We have to read and we have to listen to audio books in order to grow. There is nothing in this world we can't learn about from others. We can use their knowledge and ideas to form our own unique ideas. The human mind is capable of so much and just because we can't see it doesn't mean we should ignore it. Like our muscles, our brains must be worked also if we want to make them bigger or more defined. It all starts with one book. Reading for fifteen or twenty minutes a day can change your life forever. The more we know and understand, the more power lies within us.

5. Block Out Feed Me Morons/Negativity – The world is filled with idiots. There is no nice way around this. The world is filled with people who are jealous, insecure, and just plain ignorant. Stupid people just make life miserable—if we let them. That's why it is so important to block them out and not let their words or actions have any effect on how we live our lives. Surround yourself with great, positive people and never look back. Use social media for good and if someone is trying to penetrate your world of positivity

and greatness through social media, block them and never allow them into your world again. You will never see the greatest people in life using social media to bash people or talk trash and you know why? Because they are great! Negativity is all around us so simply know what you want and realize nothing else matters. Block out the rest of the bullshit because that is all that it is.

6. Failure is an Option – If you live your life the way you truly should, you will fail. Failing happens to the best of the best and it is what we take from that experience that ultimately determines who we are. Being great means understanding that failure happens. It is ok not to like it, but never fear it. I used to fear it more than anything and it delayed a lot of stuff for me early on, but I'm thankful for the process now. Nobody is going to go undefeated in the game of life. NOBODY! So accept failure and use it to propel you to greater accomplishments. I assure you, when you reach your goal, finally you will have an internal sense of peace and gratitude for the entire process.

7. Thank You, Thank You, Thank You – I try to start and end my day with these three words. Be grateful and appreciate life. We live in a very fast-paced world and it is easy to take things for granted. Things can change in a blink of the eye and we must be thankful for what we have and those we love. Be thankful for the journey and the ups and downs because they create the person you see in the mirror at the end of the day.

8. Be Philanthropic – We must give back in life. Just like the universe recognizes hard work, it also recognizes giving back and helping others. It doesn't have to be much; it is the thought and the effort that truly matters. If people have money to give, that is great, but it isn't the only way to give. Many homeless shelters need volunteers to help serve food or help out. There are so many great charities and organizations out there that need help. There is no better feeling than to give and help others when it truly comes from the heart. It is ok to want for ourselves, but let's never forget this rule because we are selling ourselves short if we do.

9. Enjoy Life – This is something I sometimes have a hard time applying because I am always so goal-oriented and want to be my best. Thing is, tomorrow is never guaranteed and while the odds are tomorrow will come and go, we cannot forget about today. We live in a time where it seems everybody is saying save for this, work for that, but we also have to stop and smell the roses. Otherwise, we will never be able to appreciate what we have and truly be happy. If you want to go out and party with some friends for a special occasion, well go do it. Just be smart and don't drink and drive or do anything to put yourself or anyone else in jeopardy. We need these moments in life to reward ourselves and have some fun. When we don't do this, we start living in fear of never having enough or never being satisfied. It truly does come down to having balance and getting back to business when the time is right. Live, love, laugh, and bust your ass because you will eventually regret missing out on the great things life has to offer if you neglect them long enough.

EDUCATING OURSELVES TO EDUCATE OUR KIDS

This is such an important topic. If you have ever seen the movie *Idiocracy*, then you will understand what I mean. If you haven't, I highly recommend it. It is a comedy movie where the future world is so dumbed down that all the smart people have gone extinct. All the stupid people keep having more and more kids while the smart people don't have as many kids and eventually we are left with all stupid people. While this is just a movie and I don't think we would ever get anywhere near this point in real life, we do need to educate our young or else their future and ours will get worse. It is up to everyone who has kids to teach their kids all they need to know and not just depend on others or the school system. It is scary to see how many kids are left to fend for themselves simply because of bad parenting. If you had a bad childhood or parents who were maybe not the greatest, break the cycle and give your kids the right upbringing. We have to strive to learn all that we can about things we can directly pass down to our youth, such as how to deal with money. With so much information available online, there is no reason for us not to at least be trying. You don't have to be religious to teach your kids great moral values and how being a good person will make their lives drastically better than being a bad person. The following list is things I feel all of us should teach our kids. If you aren't well versed in a particular area, find someone who is.

Love – Love all people, animals, and living creatures on this planet. It is the most powerful force in this universe and it will bring great happiness.

Respect – Respect others and understand what being a good human being means.

Manners – Know how and when to act in different situations. Knowing their surroundings and the detrimental effects of misbehaving in the wrong environment.

Importance of Family – Understand the importance of having good people you love and care about around you, whether it is your biological family, someone else, or you are starting your own family.

Honesty – Tell the truth. More pain comes from lies than the truth.

Value of Hard Work – No matter what they choose to do, nothing can replace a great work ethic. Giving their best effort will be very rewarding, and they will be admired by all.

Money and Our Money System – How money works in our world today. Financial education is a main priority and should be treated as such for our youth moving forward.

Gratitude – Thankfulness is something we all need more of in our lives. Learning to not only say thank you but *feel* thank you. You can never be too thankful in life.

Positivity – Understand that having a positive mindset will always get you further than a negative mindset. Negativity happens regardless, but the quicker we can refocus to positive, the better.

Determination – Always stay hungry and never get too high or too low.

Setting Goals – The value of knowing what you want and writing it down to remind yourself. The sooner kids realize this powerful tool, the sooner they realize they have control over their lives.

Learning and Applying – Never stop learning. Apply what they learn to their lives. Understand we all learn differently and find the way that they learn best.

The Laws of Our Country – Understand the rules that are in place, which were instituted for our protection and survival. Even if we don't agree with everything, we have to understand and respect it.

Surrounding Yourself with Good Quality People – Teaching our kids the importance of quality friends and people. Putting ourselves around negative people who are a bad influence is counterproductive to a healthy balanced life.

Sexual Health – The birds and the bees. Sex is something so many people get weird about and it is because past generations set these restrictions. Teach them the logistics, but also to respect sex and never judge other people's sexual choices. We control our future today and this is something far too many people neglect.

There are so many things for us to teach our youth, but this list will give any child the tools needed to go on in life. Maybe some of you will agree with this list and some of you may not; that is ok. The main thing to take away is that you need to determine what it is you want to pass down. We control the way the world will think tomorrow with the values we instill in our children. Don't let our screwed-up past and absurd prejudices be carried on; it has to come to an end. We created this mess and we can fix it, but it starts with each and every one of us and what we pass on. Let's make a difference and make this world the amazing place it should be!

OUR SURROUNDINGS

Earlier in the book, I mentioned that we are who we surround ourselves with, and while I believe this to be true for the most part, I should elaborate on it. If you are a positive-minded, good person, yet you are constantly around negative people who are involved with drugs and illegal activities, that doesn't mean you are that exact way. Chances are, though, you are not living up to your full potential. I feel many of us are uncomfortable being alone for any significant period of time, and this is a problem. It is understandable, as we are meant to be around other energy; there is a reason why they put people in solitary confinement when they are being severely punished. Being alone can absolutely suck if you are not comfortable with it. I feel it is absolutely critical for us to learn how to manage spending time alone so that we don't feel forced into hanging out with the wrong people just to avoid being by ourselves.

First, we must know who we are as individuals and then make sure the people who are around us have more positives attributes than negative. If you are preparing for your first fitness competition or bodybuilding contest, or you are trying to make weight for a fight, and you are around people who are constantly eating junk and making poor food choices, you are increasing your chances of not sticking to your diet. If you are someone who enjoys reading in your spare time and you are constantly around people who think reading is stupid, that probably isn't the right fit. If you work out with someone who is always cutting corners in the gym and doesn't push themselves, chances are that is going to bring you down as well. There is a saying that we are only as strong as our weakest link. I'm not advocating that we eliminate people we care about from our lives. But we have to recognize our goals and balance our friends appropriately. If your workout partner sucks, find other things you could do together and work out alone or find a partner who matches or exceeds your intensity. If your friends are affecting your food choices, find things to do with them where food isn't the main priority. If you find it hard to read around certain non-reading friends, find another time to read. It is about making adjustments based on what we know about our friends, as well as surrounding ourselves with the right quality people.

The important thing is to be conscious of your surroundings and the people you are around. From there you can start making adjustments and attracting the right people into your life. If there are people you are on the fence about, make a list of the positives and negatives of that person and decide if they are worth it or not. If someone is a true friend, they will always respect your decision to do what is best for you and your life. The key here is for you to respect your life and to do what is in your best interest because nobody else is going to do that for you.

How do you know if the people around you are good or bad? I think it is very important for the people we surround ourselves with to have several key qualities. The first quality is that they are a good human beings and treat other people well. The second thing to look for is whether that person has a sense of humor and can laugh at themselves. Life can be very serious at times, but we have to be able to laugh and have fun. The third quality is having a sense of goals and the desire to want more from life. Not everyone is going to know what they want from A to Z, but if they are aware of goals and want more in life, they are on a much better track than those that don't. People who share these three qualities make good friends. The universe is huge and life is too short to spend it with the wrong people, so get aware of your surroundings and start living your ideal life!

SELLING

Life revolves around selling. We are constantly selling, whether we know it or not. I am selling you on my thoughts and beliefs in this book, for example. When you go on a date with someone, you are selling yourself to that person to try to convince them to see you again or to have sex with you and possibly even to spend the rest of their lives with you. When I am in a wrestling ring with another performer, we are constantly selling ourselves to increase our value and to get you to be more emotionally invested in us. When you walk into a car dealership, you are swarmed by people trying to sell you on themselves and their products. When we are growing, our parents or whoever is raising us is selling us on their beliefs. Ultimately, any situation you can think of involves selling. When this was first brought to my attention, it was an eye opener. If we can truly understand this, it can help us out in important situations. For example, in a job interview, no matter what the job, big or small, if we understand we are selling ourselves to this employer, it can help us better prepare and present ourselves so we can get the job. Selling is life and the better we get at selling, the better our chances for living the life we want. But remember to be genuine and honest and have compassion for others while selling. A wonderful piece of advice by Dr. Tom Prichard, whom I think very highly of, is, "Fake it till you make it" and those words have stuck with me from the moment I first heard them. When we are selling ourselves to someone or an audience of people, it is great to be as prepared as possible and have all your ammo ready to go. Guess what, though? Sometimes you don't need to fire any bullets, and just the illusion of the gun itself is enough for people to believe! Whether it is confidence or something else you are faking, you will find it will help produce the real thing over time. Carry yourself with confidence at all the right times and you will be a master of selling!

SUCCESS TAKES TIME, EVEN FOR THE WORLD'S BEST

Success is often the result of many difficult years and failure upon failure. Success is the result of hard work, determination, and staying hungry even after failing. It can come at any time if the mindset is right and the stars are aligned, but the bigger the goal or dream, the less likely that it will happen overnight. If we look at some of the most successful people in the world, their stories are very uplifting, yet quite similar in regards to their failures early on. Albert Einstein didn't speak until he was four years old and was often bullied by other kids growing up. He didn't let that stop him! Abraham Lincoln lost seven political races and went bankrupt, and his family was evicted from their home. He didn't let that stop him! Doctor Seuss's first children's book was rejected 27—yes, 27—times by publishers. He didn't let that stop him! Walt Disney was fired from a newspaper for, of all things, not having good ideas. He didn't let that stop him! The key to take away from this, besides the fact that all these men are amazing, is that if you believe in something and know you can achieve that goal, never stop going after it until you make it happen. Results aren't always what we want, but if we keep the correct mindset, we can take a positive out of any situation and use it to motivate us to our next result.

Personally, I have achieved so many goals and it is very frustrating that the only ones I have had trouble achieving have been work (wrestling) related. I spent the last five years killing myself and bettering myself and I truly believe in my work ethic and the results it provided in and out of the ring. The problem was that I did not have control of those results or opportunities and needed to take matters into my own hands if any progress was going to be made. It came down to realizing I needed to leave the environment I was in, as it was very destructive for me. I have not given up on those goals one bit, but I am taking a different approach, one that many wouldn't have the courage to do. Some might say walking away from a three-year, 1.6 million dollar contract is, as I would say, "STUPID." I don't see it that way at all and I truly believe I will make much more than that working for myself and not being creatively restricted and used. Hell, I will use myself until I have nothing else to give because that is the type of man I am. Also, I have many other ambitions and desires that I need time to focus on, so I am very proud of my decision not to return to my former workplace. We have to be able to see the bigger picture and sometimes that means taking chances.

The key is to ignore the doubters and the negative people on social media and just keep doing what you know you can do! There is a song I absolutely love by Aaliyah called "Try Again." I first heard it as a kid, and it just always stayed with me. I play it whenever I need a pick-me-up. It reminds me to keep moving, even if it isn't at the pace I want. There are many stories of successful people out there who overcame unreal obstacles and one of them could be yours if you want it badly enough. So like Nike says, Just Do It!

PAIN AND PLEASURE

Everything we do in life is either to gain pleasure or to avoid pain. You are probably saying to yourself, "Surely, there is more to it than that, Big Guy!" When you stop and really think about it, though, and assess the things you do in your life, you will see that it comes down to these two feelings. Why does a woman spend so much time getting ready for a nice night out? To feel good about herself and possibly get compliments thus gaining pleasure. When we brush our teeth and floss at night, we do so to avoid getting cavities and other oral health issues, which would thus cause us pain. If you have a dog and you take them for walks you do so because it gives you and your dog pleasure and exercise, but also to keep your dog healthy so they don't become overweight, which could cause health issues and pain. Maybe those aren't your exact reasons, but when you break down what you are doing in your life and write down the main things, it is quite revealing. We feel either attracted to or repelled by everything we encounter, and I feel it is very important for us to recognize this. For how we feel towards something determines the decisions we make and the actions that follow. Our interpretation of each experience has caused us either pleasure or pain or both and affected our psyche, and a lifetime of this resulted in who we are at this very moment. What brings one person pain may bring another person pleasure. When things in our life that once brought us pleasure start bringing us pain, we have to look in the mirror and ask ourselves why are we still doing this thing that isn't good for us anymore.

Wrestling had always given me pleasure, and I truly appreciated and respected the art and illusion that went into telling a great story in the ring and being a larger-than-life cartoon character. I used to love going to work and seeing my hard work pay off. It was an incredible feeling! Eventually, though, being on the road four to five days a week and going on extended trips to other countries and wrestling twelve nights in a row when you are already banged up gets old real fast. It isn't like traveling for a vacation. Only being home for a day and a half, during which time you have to unpack and pack again, do your laundry, and get in a workout or two before going back for the week, leaves very little time for anything. I enjoyed this grind and actually loved the hard work, but eventually the political aspects of the job started slowly eating away at my soul. The job was no longer fun and the pleasure slowly turned to pain. It is funny how the human mind, body, and soul will start to let you know when this process is happening and the moment I felt it, I started preparing for a life outside of that environment. There are so many things in life that bring me pleasure, and hard work and dedication to being my best makes me feel good when I get results over time. I love wrestling and will always continue to do it, but at this point, it was an easy decision to walk away from the environment I was in. The goal for us all is to be aware, so sit down and make a list of the things you do and don't do in your life and why. Doing so can be a real eye opener and help you make some positive adjustments in your life!

WHATEVER YOUR JOB, GIVE IT YOUR ALL

For as long as I can remember, I have always had a strong work ethic, no matter what the job or activity was. I don't know if it was just the way I was born or if it was instilled in me at a young age, but I am very thankful for it. In elementary school, I won awards for best athlete and best sportsmanship. I don't think at that age I was anything special, but no matter what sport or activity we played, I always gave it everything I had and had fun interacting with all of the other kids. Do I think there were better athletes than me out there? Most definitely. I wasn't the best at everything, but I was my best and did my best! My fifth grade year, my classmates wanted me to run for president of our school (J.T. McWilliams Jets) and I hadn't the slightest clue about school politics. I didn't care, though. I ran and I put my best effort forward in learning what it was the school and kids wanted, and I went out and won president of our school. Fast-forward to middle school, and I won athlete of the year for our physical education class and, again, it was just because I applied myself and showed up each day loving life, being happy, and having fun. There were many exceptional athletes in this school (R.O. Gibson) and it was just a matter of wanting to be my best in anything I put my effort into. The following year I worked in the school cafeteria. I got to eat free for working in there and I put on quite a bit of not-so-good weight from their monster French fries and ranch dipping sauces. I just showed up each day and worked as hard as I could, staying focused and trying to be of service to the adults who did that for a living. At the end of the year at our awards ceremony, I was presented with a Cafeteria Worker of the Year award. It was the first time in the school's history that they created an award for the cafeteria. I thought it was hilarious at the time, not really seeing the significance of it, but looking back, I am as proud of this award as anything I have done. That work ethic I laughed at that day is the sole reason I am who I am in life. I am not the greatest this or that, I am just the greatest me in things I do and that has provided me with great results.

Fast-forward to a 22-year-old me trying out for WWE Tough Enough, a reality TV show from 2004 where eight finalists were chosen to compete for a WWE contract (at the time, my dream job). One hundred of the top finalists were chosen to compete in a two-day tryout at Venice Beach. Day one was extremely tough and there was a military-style obstacle course that was classified as a level 5, I believe on a scale of 1 to 10. Mind you, day two would be the level 10 course. I was in great shape, but this obstacle course was in the sand, and I did not pace myself. Guys were getting carried away on stretchers and being put on oxygen masks afterwards. The course was ripping people apart and they had boot camp instructors at strategic points to bust your balls when they saw you getting fatigued. Finally, it was my turn and for the first three-quarters of this obstacle course, I fucking owned it. I went as hard as I could from the first step and never looked back. Well that would normally be ok except this was in the sand and I had not prepared for the sudden loss of feeling in my legs! Out of nowhere, my body hit a wall and I started collapsing. Cue those damn boot camp instructors. They saw me hit that wall and they were all over my Big-Guy-in-training ass. I kept trying to get to my feet and kept falling on my face, as no matter how hard I tried, I couldn't stand on my jelly legs. I had never been in this position before in my life and all that kept going through my mind was I would never be able to look myself in the mirror or look at my family if I just gave up on my dreams facedown in the sand! I had a quarter of the way to go to finish and somehow I pulled myself up and willed myself to that finish line. I didn't have the best time of the day, but that effort got me to day two of the tryout in the top 25. Where others had quit, I had kept going, and to this day, it is one of my proudest moments. Day two I showed up and kicked ass, as I paced myself better on the twice-as-difficult course. This pattern has been similar my entire life. Such as when I got released from WWE and got a job in Louisville, KY, at Smokey Bones BBQ Restaurant. I worked twelve-hour days and holidays, morning to night, to pay the bills. Not in a million years would I have thought I would have that job as my sole source of income. It was very difficult to swallow my pride when people were rude and talked down to me because they saw me as just a server. Guess what, though? I busted my ass morning to night and I made that damn job fun for myself and everyone else around me. I brought the energy that I have inside of me, and I am so proud of myself for that. The manager at that time, whom we called Jimbo Slice as he was a huge Kimbo Slice fan, told me I was the best server he had ever had. Again, I'm sure there were better, but I just worked hard and gave that job the same effort I did in anything else in life, even if it was just a job serving people and the money wasn't always good.

That is why I feel it is important for us to understand that we are all important, no matter what our jobs or titles. It doesn't matter if we are flipping burgers, cleaning toilets, or are president of The United States of America. No matter what our job, if we show up each day and work our asses off and try to make it fun, it will be significantly better than if we just half ass it. Who knows, one day you could be flipping burgers balls to the wall, and the restaurant is clean because in between you are paying attention to small details and cleaning this and that. Maybe you are having fun, laughing with the other employees while still focusing on your job 100 percent and everything is just flowing and time is flying by because you are having fun. It just so happens the district manager is in the restaurant that day undercover, seeing how things are going on a typical day, and he sees this one guy and how hard he works and how his energy makes everyone else that much better. You just working hard doing the right thing could be all it takes for that district manager to say I want this guy in our manager training program ASAP. That kind of work ethic and attitude is what we want leading our stores. Fast-forward ten years and that burger flipper could be owner of his very own franchise or even ten of them! It doesn't matter what our jobs are, if we set goals and work hard, we can turn around situations that aren't ideal. It is just a matter of having that inner motivation. Sure, situations could help trigger that inner motivation, like, say, having a child and a family that you have to support, but making that choice still comes from within. So no matter what you do and what your situation in life is, whatever it is you are doing, just do your best and give it your all. I promise you, the upside to doing this always outweighs the downside!

THE IMPORTANCE OF COLORS

Colors are all around us and play a big part in our moods and every color has its own language. Color in essence is a form of nonverbal communication. Before going further, let's take a look at some of the colors and their meanings. Thanks to <u>empower-yourself-with-color-psychology.com</u> for the meanings behind the colors (reprinted with permission).

RED:

Red is the color of energy, passion, action, ambition, and determination. It is also the color of anger and sexual passion. This color is a warm and positive color associated with our most physical needs and our will to survive. It exudes a strong and powerful masculine energy. Red is energizing. It excites the emotions and motivates us to take action. It signifies a pioneering spirit and leadership qualities, promoting ambition and determination. It is also strong-willed and can give confidence to those who are shy or lacking in willpower. Being the color of physical movement, the color red awakens our physical life force. It is the color of sexuality and can stimulate deeper and more intimate passions in us, such as love and sex on the positive side or revenge and anger on the negative. It is often used to express love, as in Valentine's Day, however it relates more to sexuality and lust, rather than love—love is expressed with pink. At its most positive, it can create life with its sexual energy, or use its negative expression of anger and aggression to fuel war and destruction. The color red can stimulate the appetite, often being used in restaurants for this purpose. It also increases cravings for food and other stimuli. Being surrounded by too much of the color red can cause us to become irritated, agitated, and ultimately angry. Too little and we become cautious, manipulative and fearful. In Eastern cultures such as China, red is the color for good luck. Although times are changing and many Chinese brides now wear white, it is traditionally the color for weddings. In Indian culture, it symbolizes purity and is often used in their wedding gowns.

ORANGE:

Orange is the color of social communication and optimism. From a negative color, meaning it is also a sign of pessimism and superficiality. The color orange radiates warmth and happiness, combining the physical energy and stimulation of red with the cheerfulness of yellow. Orange relates to 'gut reaction' or our gut instincts, as opposed to the physical reaction of red or the mental reaction of yellow. Orange offers emotional strength in difficult times. It helps us to bounce back from disappointments and despair, assisting in recovery from grief. The color psychology of orange is optimistic and uplifting, rejuvenating our spirit. In fact orange is so optimistic and uplifting that we should all find ways to use it in our everyday life, even if it is just an orange colored pen that we use. Orange brings spontaneity and a positive outlook on life and is a great color to use during tough economic times, keeping us motivated and helping us to look on the bright side of life. With its enthusiasm for life, the color orange relates to adventure and risk-taking, inspiring physical confidence, competition, and independence. Those inspired by orange are always on the go! In relation to the meaning of colors, orange is extroverted and uninhibited, often encouraging exhibitionism or, at the very least, showing off! The color orange relates to social communication, stimulating two-way conversations. A warm and inviting color, it is both physically and mentally stimulating, so it gets people thinking and talking! At the same time, orange is also stimulating to the appetite. If you love having people around the kitchen table, orange will keep them talking and eating for a long time. Many restaurants use pastel versions of orange, such as apricot or peach or deeper versions such as terracotta, for their décor as they are more subtle than red, yet still increase the appetite and promote conversation and social interaction, which in turn encourages patrons to have a good time and to eat and drink more. The color orange is obviously the worst color to have in the kitchen if you are trying to lose weight! Orange aids in the assimilation of new ideas and frees the spirit of its limitations, giving us the freedom to be ourselves. At the same time, it encourages self-respect and respect of others. Orange is probably the most rejected and underused color of our time. However, young people do respond well to it as it has a degree of youthful impulsiveness to it.

YELLOW:

Yellow is the color of the mind and the intellect. It is optimistic and cheerful. However, it can also suggest impatience, criticism, and cowardice. This color relates to acquired knowledge. It is the color which resonates with the left or logic side of the brain, stimulating our mental faculties and creating mental agility and perception. Being the lightest hue of the spectrum, the color psychology of yellow is uplifting and illuminating, offering hope, happiness, cheerfulness, and fun. In the meaning of colors, yellow inspires original thought and inquisitiveness. Yellow is creative from a mental aspect, the color of new ideas, helping us to find new ways of doing things. It is the practical thinker, not the dreamer. Yellow is the best color to create enthusiasm for life and can awaken greater confidence and optimism. The color yellow loves a challenge, particularly a mental challenge. Within the meaning of colors, yellow is the great communicator and loves to talk. Yellow is the color of the networker and the journalist, all working and communicating on a mental level. Yellow is the scientist, constantly analyzing, looking at both sides before making a decision; methodical and decisive. Yellow is the entertainer, the comic, the clown. Yellow helps with decision-making as it relates to clarity of thought and ideas, although it can often be impulsive. Yellow helps us focus, study, and recall information, useful during exam time. The color yellow can be anxiety producing as it is fast moving and can cause us to feel agitated. Yellow has a tendency to make you more mentally analytical and critical—this includes being self-critical as well as critical of others. Yellow is non-emotional, coming from the head rather than the heart. Yellow depends on itself, preferring to not get emotionally involved. Yellow is related to the ego and our sense of self-worth, to how we feel about ourselves and how we are perceived by others. Yellow is the most highly visible of all colors which is why it is used for pedestrian crossings. Take note of the crossings which are marked in white—they are less easy to see than those marked yellow, particularly on wet and cloudy days. If you are going through a lot of change in your life, you may find you can't tolerate the color yellow very well—this will usually pass. It just means that you are having trouble coping with all the changes at the moment and yellow vibrates too fast for you, making you feel stressed. Introduce green or a soft orange into your life for a while to balance and restore your energies. Many older people don't respond well to large amounts of yellow because it vibrates too fast for them.

GREEN:

Green is the color of balance and growth. It can mean both self-reliance as a positive and possessiveness as a negative, amongst many other meanings. This is the color of balance and harmony. From a color psychology perspective, it is the great balancer of the heart and the emotions, creating equilibrium between the head and the heart. From a meaning of colors perspective, green is also the color of growth, the color of spring, of renewal and rebirth. It renews and restores depleted energy. It is the sanctuary away from the stresses of modern living, restoring us back to a sense of well-being. This is why there is so much of this relaxing color on the earth, and why we need to keep it that way. Green is an emotionally positive color, giving us the ability to love and nurture ourselves and others unconditionally. A natural peacemaker, it must avoid the tendency to become a martyr. It loves to observe, and therefore relates to the counselor, the good listener, the social worker. It loves to contribute to society. It is the charity worker, the good parent and the helpful neighbor. Being a combination of yellow and blue, green encompasses the mental clarity and optimism of yellow with the emotional calm and insight of blue, inspiring hope and a generosity of spirit not available from other colors. This is a color that has a strong sense of right or wrong, inviting good judgment. It sees both sides of the equation, weighs them up, and then usually takes the moral stand in making appropriate decisions. On the negative side, it can be judgmental and over-cautious. Green promotes a love of nature and a love of family, friends, pets, and the home. It is the color of the garden lover, the home lover, and the good host. It is generous and loves to share, but it also looks for recognition. It is friendly and can keep confidences. This color relates to stability and endurance, giving us persistence and the strength to cope with adversity. Green is the color of prosperity and abundance, of finance and material wealth. It relates to the business world, to real estate and property. Prosperity gives a feeling of safety to green. On the negative, the color green can be possessive and materialistic, with a need to own people and things.

BLUE:

Blue is the color of trust and peace. It can suggest loyalty and integrity as well as conservatism and frigidity. This color is one of trust, honesty, and loyalty. It is sincere, reserved, and quiet, and doesn't like to make a fuss or draw attention. It hates confrontation, and likes to do things in its own way. From a color psychology perspective, blue is reliable and responsible. This color exhibits an inner security and confidence. You can rely on it to take control and do the right thing in difficult times. It has a need for order and direction in its life, including its living and work spaces. This is a color that seeks peace and tranquility above everything else, promoting both physical and mental relaxation. It reduces stress, creating a sense of calmness, relaxation, and order—we certainly feel a sense of calm if we lie on our backs and look into a bright blue cloudless sky. It slows the metabolism. The paler the blue the more freedom we feel. In the meaning of colors, blue relates to one-to-one communication, especially communication using the voice—speaking the truth through verbal self-expression; it is the teacher, the public speaker. The color blue is idealistic, enhancing self-expression and our ability to communicate our needs and wants. It inspires higher ideals. Blue's wisdom comes from its higher level of intelligence, a spiritual perspective. Blue is the color of the spirit, devotion, and religious study. It enhances contemplation and prayer. On the other hand, blue's devotion can be to any cause or concept it believes in, including devotion to family or work. Blue is the helper, the rescuer, the friend in need. Its success is defined by the quality and quantity of its relationships. It is a giver, not a taker. It likes to build strong trusting relationships and becomes deeply hurt if that trust is betrayed. Blue is conservative and predictable, a safe and non-threatening color, and the most universally liked color of all, probably because it is safe and non-threatening. At the same time blue is persistent and determined to succeed in whichever endeavors it pursues. Change is difficult for blue. It is inflexible and when faced with a new or different idea, it considers it, analyzes it, thinks it over slowly, and then tries to make it fit its own acceptable version of reality. Blue is nostalgic. It is a color that lives in the past, relating everything in the present and the future to experiences in the past.

INDIGO:

Indigo is the color of intuition. In the meaning of colors, it can mean idealism and structure as well as ritualistic and addictive. The color indigo is the color of intuition and perception and is helpful in opening the third eye. It promotes deep concentration during times of introspection and meditation, helping you achieve deeper levels of consciousness. It is a color which relates to the "New Age"—the ability to use the Higher Mind to see beyond the normal senses with great powers of perception. It relies on intuition rather than gut feeling. Indigo is a deep midnight blue. It is a combination of deep blue and violet and holds the attributes of both these colors. Service to humanity is one of the strengths of the color indigo. Powerful and dignified, indigo conveys integrity and deep sincerity. The color meaning of indigo reflects great devotion, wisdom, and justice along with fairness and impartiality. It is a defender of people's rights to the end. Structure creates identity and meaning for indigo. In fact, an indigo person cannot function without structure—it throws them right off balance. Organization is very important to them and they can be quite inflexible when it comes to order in their lives. Indigo loves rituals and traditions, religion and the institutional system, conforming to things that have worked in the past while planning for the future. Indigo stimulates right brain or creative activity and helps with spatial skills. It is a dramatic color relating to the world of the theater, which, during times of stress, becomes the drama queen, making a mountain out of a molehill! The negative color meaning of indigo relates to fanaticism and addiction. Its addiction encompasses everything from a need for recognized qualifications to a need for illegal drugs, from the workaholic to the religious fanatic. Indigo can be narrow-minded, intolerant and prejudiced.

PURPLE:

Purple is the color of the imagination. It can be creative and individual or immature and impractical. This color relates to the imagination and spirituality. It stimulates the imagination and inspires high ideals. It is an introspective color, allowing us to get in touch with our deeper thoughts. The difference between violet and purple is that violet appears in the visible light spectrum, or rainbow, whereas purple is simply a mix of red and blue. Violet has the highest vibration in the visible spectrum. While the violet is not quite as intense as purple, its essence is similar. Generally, the names are interchangeable and the meaning of the colors is similar. Both contain the energy and strength of red with the spirituality and integrity of blue. This is the union of body and soul creating a balance between our physical and our spiritual energies. Purple or violet assists those who seek the meaning of life and spiritual fulfillment—it expands our awareness, connecting us to a higher consciousness. For this reason, it is associated with transformation of the soul and the philosophers of the world are often attracted to it. In the meaning of colors, purple and violet represent the future, the imagination, and dreams, while spiritually calming the emotions. They inspire and enhance psychic ability and spiritual enlightenment, while, at the same time, keeping us grounded. The color violet relates to the fantasy world, and a need to escape from the practicalities of life. It is the daydreamer escaping from reality. From a color psychology perspective, purple and violet promote harmony of the mind and the emotions, contributing to mental balance and stability, peace of mind, a link between the spiritual and the physical worlds, between thought and activity. Violet and purple support the practice of meditation. The color violet inspires unconditional and selfless love, devoid of ego, encouraging sensitivity and compassion. Violet can be sensitive to all the different forms of pollution in the world today, whether it be air pollution, noise pollution, visual pollution or the pollution in our food chain. This sensitivity makes violet susceptible to illness and allergies, vulnerable to its everyday surroundings. Violet encourages creative pursuits and seeks inspiration and originality through its creative endeavors. It likes to be unique, individual and independent, not one of the crowd. Artists, musicians, writers, poets, and psychics are all inspired by violet and its magic and mystery. Violet is the color of the humanitarian, using its better judgment to do good for others. Combining wisdom and power with sensitivity and humility, violet can achieve a lot for those less fortunate. The color purple is specifically associated with royalty and the nobility, creating an impression of luxury, wealth, and extravagance. Purple has power. It has a richness and quality to it that demands respect. Purple is ambitious and self-assured, the leader. Too much of the color purple can promote or aggravate depression in some. It is one color that should be used extremely carefully and in small amounts by those who are vulnerable to these depressed states.

TURQUOISE:

The color meaning of turquoise is communication and clarity of mind. It can also be impractical and idealistic. Turquoise helps to open the lines of communication between the heart and the spoken word. It presents as a friendly and happy color enjoying life. In color psychology, turquoise controls and heals the emotions creating emotional balance and stability. In the process, it can appear to be on an emotional roller coaster, up and down, until it balances itself. A combination of blue and a small amount of yellow, it fits in on the color scale between green and blue. It radiates the peace, calm, and tranquility of blue and the balance and growth of green with the uplifting energy of yellow. This is a color that recharges our spirits during times of mental stress and tiredness, alleviating feelings of loneliness. You only have to focus on the color turquoise, whether on a wall or clothing and you feel instant calm and gentle invigoration, ready to face the world again! It is a great color to have around you, particularly in an emergency, as it helps with clear thinking and decision-making. It assists in the development of organizational and management skills. It influences rather than preaching and demanding. This is a good color to aid concentration and clarity of thought for public speakers as it calms the nervous system, gives control over speech and expression, and builds confidence. Print your speech notes on turquoise and every time you glance down you will feel the effects of the color. It heightens levels of creativity and sensitivity; it is good at multi-tasking, becoming bored if forced to focus on one thing only. Sometimes thinking can become scattered if surrounded by too much of this balancing color. Turquoise encourages inner healing through its ability to enhance empathy and caring. It heightens our intuitive ability and opens the door to spiritual growth. It is the color of the evolved soul. The color turquoise can also be self-centered, tuning in to its own needs above all others. At the same time, it can help us to build our self-esteem and to love ourselves, which in turn supports our ability to love others unconditionally. At its most extreme, it can be boastful and narcissistic. Although it is self-sufficient, it fears being alone and can become aloof and unapproachable when this occurs, making the situation worse. Turquoise has strong powers of observation and perception and can be quite discriminating. It has the ability to identify the way forward, the way to success, balancing the pros and cons, the right and wrong, of any situation. It is a good color to use when you are stuck in a rut and don't know which way to move. This is a color that can sometimes be impractical and idealistic and remote from emotional reactions, appearing excessively cool, calm, and collected. Too much of this color in your life may give you an overactive mind and create emotional imbalance, making you either over-emotional or non-emotional. Too little turquoise in your life may cause you to withhold your emotions, resulting in secrecy and confusion about your direction in life. From a negative perspective, the meaning of the color turquoise relates to being either over-emotional or non-emotional, lacking communication skills, being unreliable and deceptive.

PINK:

The color psychology of pink is unconditional love and nurturing. Pink can also be immature, silly and girlish. This color represents compassion, nurturing, and love. It relates to unconditional love and understanding, and the giving and receiving of nurturing. A combination of red and white, pink contains the need for action of red, helping it to achieve the potential for success and insight offered by white. It is the passion and power of red softened with the purity, openness, and completeness of white. The deeper the pink, the more passion and energy it exhibits. Pink is feminine and romantic, affectionate and intimate, thoughtful and caring. It tones down the physical passion of red, replacing it with a gentle loving energy. Pink is intuitive and insightful, showing tenderness and kindness with its empathy and sensitivity. In color psychology, pink is a sign of hope. It is a positive color inspiring warm and comforting feelings, a sense that everything will be okay. Pink calms and reassures our emotional energies, alleviating feelings of anger, aggression, resentment, abandonment, and neglect. Studies have confirmed that exposure to large amounts of pink can have a calming effect on the nerves and create physical weakness in people. Violent and aggressive prisoners have been successfully calmed by placing them in a pink room for a specified amount of time. Exposure for too long can have the opposite effect. The color pink puts people in touch with the nurturing side of themselves, through either the need to receive or the need to give nurturing and TLC (tender loving care!). Be aware of this if you have a friend who constantly wears pink as it may indicate a need for acceptance, support, and unconditional love! Pink is a non-threatening color seeking appreciation, respect and admiration. It doesn't like to be taken for granted and just loves to hear the words 'thank you.' Pink can signify good health, being 'in the pink,' and success as in 'everything's rosy.' The color pink represents the sweetness and innocence of the child in all of us. It is the color of uncomplicated emotions, inexperience, and naiveté. A constant and exclusive use of pink can often lead you to become immature, silly, and girlish, abandoning your adult responsibilities. Pink can also remind you of earlier childhood memories, associated with nurturing and comfort from your mother or a mother figure. Pink, from a negative color meaning, can represent a lack of willpower, a lack of self-reliance, and a lack of self-worth. It can indicate an overly emotional and overly cautious nature. Combining pink with other darker colors such as dark blue, dark green, black or gray, adds strength and sophistication to pink.

MAGENTA:

In the meaning of colors, magenta is a color of universal harmony and emotional balance. It is spiritual yet practical, encouraging common sense and a balanced outlook on life. This is a color that helps to create harmony and balance in every aspect of life; physically, mentally, emotionally, and spiritually. A combination of red and violet, magenta contains the passion, power, and energy of red, restrained by the introspection and quiet energy of violet. Magenta influences our whole personal and spiritual development. It strengthens our intuition and psychic ability while assisting us to rise above the everyday dramas of our daily life to experience a greater level of awareness and knowledge. This color is an instrument of change and transformation; it helps to release old emotional patterns that prevent personal and spiritual development and aids us in moving forward. Magenta is uplifting to our spirits during times of unhappiness, anger, or frustration. In the meaning of colors, magenta represents universal love at its highest level. It promotes compassion, kindness, and cooperation and encourages a sense of self-respect and contentment in those who use it. Gentle and caring in its approach, it generates acceptance, tolerance, support, and patience. The color magenta is a color of cheerfulness, happiness, contentment, and appreciation for what you have acquired and achieved. Most people feel more optimistic when in the company of magenta. Magenta is the color of the non-conformist, the free spirit. It pushes you to take responsibility for creating your own path in life and increases dream activity while assisting you in turning your ambitions and desires into reality. A strong and inspiring color, magenta can appear outrageous and shocking on one hand or innovative and imaginative on the other. It is creativity inspired by beauty. Magenta is spontaneous and impulsive, yet resourceful and organized. It is invaluable in negotiating peace and calm in those who are at odds with one another. From a negative perspective, magenta can promote depression and despair in some, and prevent others from dealing with challenges—it may be just too relaxing for introverts and the chronically depressed. Being surrounded by too much magenta energy can generate arrogance and bossiness, making us feel overwhelmed, irritated, anxious, and intolerant. An excess of magenta energy can be balanced by introducing green into your surroundings.

BROWN:

The color brown is a friendly yet serious, down-to-earth color that relates to security, protection, comfort, and material wealth. The color brown is a serious, down-to-earth color signifying stability, structure, and support. Relating to the protection and support of the family unit, with a keen sense of duty and responsibility, brown takes its obligations seriously. It encourages a strong need for security and a sense of belonging, with family and friends being of utmost importance. In the meaning of colors, brown is the color of material security and the accumulation of material possessions. The color brown relates to quality in everything—a comfortable home, the best food and drink and loyal companionship. It is a color of physical comfort, simplicity, and quality. From a negative perspective, it can also give the impression of cheapness and stinginess in certain circumstances. Brown is friendly and approachable. It is loyal, trustworthy, and dependable in a practical and realistic way. In color psychology, brown is honest, genuine, and sincere. It relates to the hardworking, the industrious and reliable, with both feet planted firmly on the ground. It is sensual, sensitive, and warm, engulfing one in a feeling of calmness and comfort. It is a practical and sensible color which implies common sense. It hides the dirt! The color brown is associated with wholesome, natural, and organic produce and anything related to the great outdoors, agriculture, and farming. Brown is a frugal color—it is not associated with frivolity, excess or waste in any form. While it is materialistic, it values quality above all else, and everything in moderation. Some browns can show a degree of sophistication or elegance, depending on other colors associated with the brown. For example, brown with a soft white or ivory can appear stylish and classy, although more casual than black with soft white or ivory. Brown suppresses the emotions, creating a safe haven from the stresses of the outside world within which problems can be contemplated and solved. Brown is a color of structure, although by no means does it encourage perfectionism—rather it encourages orderliness and organization. The color brown gives reassurance. It is quietly confident but never the life of the party! Brown does not seek attention—it prefers to stay in the background, allowing other colors around it to shine. Brown is solid with strength and maturity. It prefers to function in its own safe little world—it is not carefree and spontaneous and doesn't like surprises. It can be considered dull, boring, and unexciting by many. In fact, it is one of the least preferred colors in the western world, along with orange and yellow. Brown is a predominant color on the planet, along with green. Brown is comforting and stabilizing, while green is balancing and rejuvenating, just what we all need to help us deal with the stresses of modern life. The meaning of the color brown can vary slightly depending on the colors which are mixed together to create the brown. Brown can be a combination of black, yellow, orange, red, gray, green, blue, pink, and purple, and each of the colors in it will add a variation to the meaning.

GRAY:

The color gray is an unemotional color. It is detached, neutral, impartial and indecisive—the fence-sitter. From a color psychology perspective, gray is the color of compromise—being neither black nor white, it is the transition between two non-colors. The closer gray gets to black, the more dramatic and mysterious it becomes. The closer it gets to silver or white, the more illuminating and lively it becomes. Being both motionless and emotionless, gray is solid and stable, creating a sense of calm and composure, relief from a chaotic world. The color gray is subdued, quiet, and reserved. It does not stimulate, energize, rejuvenate, or excite. In the meaning of colors, gray is conservative, boring, drab and depressing on the one hand and elegant and formal on the other, yet never glamorous. Gray conforms—it is conventional, dependable, and practical. It is a color of maturity and responsibility, associated with the gray hair of old age. It will never be the center of attention, the dynamic leader, or the director—it is too safe and toned down. It can stifle and depress energy but it is also the stable base from which the new and positive can come. Gray is controlled. It has a steadying effect on other colors with which it comes into contact, toning down the stronger and brighter colors and illuminating the softer colors. Rarely is gray a perfect mix of black and white—it often has elements of other colors such as blue, green, pink, mauve or yellow within it which lift it and energize it. Too much of the color gray creates sadness and depression and a tendency to loneliness and isolation. Add some color to change this. Most people are indifferent to gray—it relates to the corporate worker in the gray suit—conservative, reliable, formal and independent and maybe boring.

SILVER:

The color silver has a feminine energy; it is related to the moon and the ebb and flow of the tides—it is fluid, emotional, sensitive, and mysterious. It is soothing, calming, and purifying. From a color psychology viewpoint, it signals a time of reflection and a change of direction as it illuminates the way forward. It helps with the cleansing and releasing of mental, physical, and emotional issues and blockages as it opens new doors and lights the way to the future. With its reflective and sensitive qualities, silver inspires intuition, clairvoyance, and mental telepathy. It reflects back any energy given out, whether it is positive or negative. In the meaning of colors, it is associated with prestige and wealth. It is seen as a glamorous, sophisticated color related to female energy, prosperity, and modernity. Silver restores equilibrium and stability to both feminine power and spiritual energy. It protects itself from outside negativity, reflecting the energy back to where it began. This color is very versatile, being shiny, modern and hi-tech on one hand and alluring, sparkling and elegant on the other. From a color psychology perspective, silver is respectable and courteous, dignified, self-controlled, responsible, patient, determined and organized—it relates well to the corporate world and those in positions of responsibility, whether they are male or female. In color psychology, with a balance between black and white, silver is seen as a good critic, unbiased and compassionate with a mature sense of justice. Traditionally silver represents the celebration of the 25th anniversary and is related to the graceful aging of those with silver colored hair. It is a color that works well with most other colors—it illuminates and reflects the energy of those colors which surround it. The color silver has similar energy to gray but it is more light-hearted and optimistic. From a negative aspect, silver can be indecisive and non-committal, dull and lifeless in a colorless world, neutral, cold and insincere. It can be deceptive and two-faced.

GOLD:

The color gold is the color of success, achievement, and triumph. Associated with abundance and prosperity, luxury and quality, prestige and sophistication, value and elegance, the psychology of this color implies affluence, material wealth, and extravagance. Gold in its physical state, by its very nature, denotes wealth and prestige in every country, culture, and market in the world today—it is probably the most valuable and easily traded commodity available in the global market place. This color is linked to masculine energy and the power of the sun, compared to silver, which is associated with feminine energy and the sensitivity of the moon. Optimistic and positive, gold adds richness and warmth to everything with which it is associated—it illuminates and enhances other things around it. At the uppermost level, this is a color which is associated with higher ideals, wisdom, understanding, and enlightenment. It inspires knowledge, spirituality and a deep understanding of the self and the soul. In the meaning of colors, gold is generous and giving, compassionate and loving, the benefactor or patron, sharing its wisdom, knowledge and wealth with others. Gold is the color of the winner—first place medals are always in gold, silver is second place. Confident, passionate, and eye-catching, gold draws attention to itself. Gold is a warm color that can be shiny, glistening, and happy as well as dull, muted, and traditional. The brighter shades of gold catch the eye with their brilliance while the darker muted shades are deep, warm, and intense. Gold has long been associated with royalty throughout the world, along with purple. Being surrounded by too much gold can lead you to become egotistical, self-righteous, and opportunistic in your quest for greater power and influence. If living under the negative of the color gold, you may not trust easily, have a fear of success and wealth, or even exhibit a fear of failure. You may be selfish and demanding, lacking kindness and generosity, even to the extreme of being miserly.

WHITE:

White is color at its most complete and pure, the color of perfection. The color meaning of white is purity, innocence, wholeness, and completion. In color psychology white is the color of new beginnings, wiping the slate clean, so to speak. It is the blank canvas waiting to be written upon. While white isn't stimulating to the senses, it opens the way for the creation of anything the mind can conceive. White contains an equal balance of all the colors of the spectrum, representing both the positive and negative aspects of all colors. Its basic feature is equality, implying fairness and impartiality, neutrality and independence. It is interesting to note that babies come into the world with a perfect balance of white, ready to imprint their lives with all the colors of the spectrum (hopefully!) from all their life experiences. White is totally reflective, awakening openness, growth and creativity. You can't hide behind it as it amplifies everything in its way. The color white is cleanliness personified, the ultimate in purity!! This is why it is traditionally worn by western brides, and the reason why doctors wear white jackets. White is a color of protection and encouragement, offering a sense of peace and calm, comfort and hope, helping alleviate emotional upsets. It creates a sense of order and efficiency, a great help if you need to declutter your life. White offers an inner cleansing and purifying of your thoughts, emotions and, ultimately, your spirit, refreshing and strengthening your entire energy system. While there are very few negative connotations to white, particularly in western culture, too much white can be cold, isolating, and empty. It implies a feeling of sterility, detachment, and disinterest, providing little stimulation for the senses. In other cultures it is traditionally related to death and mourning. In these cultures, death usually means the end of one life and the beginning of another, moving forward to a new life, so the color psychology meaning of new beginnings still holds. White may indicate the completion of a cycle in your life—you may find you have a desire for white clothing or white in your surroundings at a time when you are moving in a new direction in your life, for example, planning an overseas trip for the first time, or moving house after a long time in one place, or in seeking a new relationship or a new career direction. Many people use white as a recall of their youth and innocence. It reminds them of a time when their lives were easier and less complicated. White is used in many medical practices such as dental surgeries and doctors' rooms as an indication of cleanliness and efficiency; however it also can give the feeling of sterility and coldness of emotions and may lead patients to think the doctor or dentist won't relate to them on an emotional and personal level. It can be too clinical and sterile. Too much white can cause feelings of isolation and emptiness; it can be too pristine and immaculate, making you feel as though you can't make a move for fear of upsetting it or creating a mess.

BLACK:

The color black relates to the hidden, the secretive and the unknown, and as a result it creates an air of mystery. It keeps things bottled up inside, hidden from the world. In color psychology, this color gives protection from external emotional stress. It creates a barrier between itself and the outside world, providing comfort while protecting its emotions and feelings and hiding its vulnerabilities, insecurities, and lack of self-confidence. Black is the absorption of all color and the absence of light. Black hides, while white brings to light. What black covers, white uncovers. We all use black at various times to hide from the world around us in one way or another. Some of us use it to hide our weight; others amongst us use it to hide our feelings, our fears, or our insecurities. In color psychology, black means power and control, hanging on to information and things rather than giving out to others. Black is intimidating, unfriendly and unapproachable because of the power it exudes. It can prevent two-way communication because of its intimidation. The salesman wearing all black will make a lot of sales, but no friends! It radiates authority, but creates fear in the process. Black implies self-control and discipline, independence and a strong will, and giving an impression of authority and power. Black absorbs negative energy. It is useful to carry something black with you to protect you from harm and negativity when traveling or when going about your usual daily activities outside your home. People who like black may be conventional, conservative, and serious, or they may think of themselves as being sophisticated or very dignified. The color black is often seen as a color of sophistication, as in 'the little black dresses' or 'the black tie event.' Affluent and success-oriented women often choose black as it can give an impression of elegance, sophistication, and confidence.

Black is often associated with sexiness and seduction, as in the temptress in sexy black lingerie creating an air of mystery and intrigue. It can also imply submission to another (including a sexual partner), similar to the priest wearing black robes in submission to God. Black is the end, but the end always implies a new beginning. When the light appears, black becomes white, the color of new beginnings. Teenagers often have a psychological need to wear black during the stage of transition from the innocence of childhood to the sophistication of adulthood. It signifies the ending of one part of their life and the beginning of another, allowing them to hide from the world while they discover their own unique identity. It is important they go through this stage but a worry when it continues on into adult years if they continue to wear black to the exclusion of other colors. Too much black can cause depression and mood swings and create a negative environment. Combined with white only, it can create an argumentative atmosphere. It is best to use some color with black to lighten and brighten its energy.

As you can see there is a lot more meaning to color than most would assume. I guess it all makes sense now why the bad guys in wrestling wear predominantly black and the good guys wear the flashy colors, right? I remember reading about colors randomly when younger and it always fascinated me. I have since read quite a bit on the subject and it plays a part in my life from how I decorate my house to the vehicles I drive and the wrestling attire I wear. For my house, for example, I had my carpets done a deep blue as that color helps me feel calm and at peace. When I am in the confines of my kingdom, I prefer to feel calm and at peace. When I bought my truck years ago, I got a midnight blue with silver lining as that color, which is in between blue and black, gives me the power and control of black yet the calmness and tranquility of blue. For my sports car, I chose red, as that color fuels energy and excitement! As for my wrestling attire, I always try to wear colors that will stand out and usually pair a higher energy color with a calmer color, such as wearing red and blue, or purple and yellow, or green and orange. It has served me very well, as my action figures were some of the highest selling during my time in WWE, even when not used in a positive light. I truly credit a lot of that to not only my look, but the colors I wore with my customary singlet. (A funny story on that singlet. WWE owner Vince McMahon was adamant about me switching to trunks after I'd worn a singlet for over four years. I explained to him how the singlet was a canvas for me to express my emotions and that trunks don't really allow for that. To me it was like my superhero costume and after explaining this to him, he let me keep it. I did later switch to trunks to appease him temporarily, just to let him see what he was losing.) Colors will forever play a part in my life and simply having a basic understanding of them could help brighten your day!

ASK QUESTIONS

I have always enjoyed the process of figuring things out for myself, so I've stubbornly avoided asking questions. Sometimes, by not asking the right questions at the right times, I have delayed my learning by extended periods of time. I don't know where this attitude started, but I would imagine that as a kid I didn't get a favorable response from a teacher, so I thought, "Well, fuck this, I just won't ask questions." And then, in my first year in wrestling, I realized that I was going to have to ask questions, as learning the skill of being a professional wrestler doesn't just happen overnight. Being met once again with criticism and being blown off didn't set well with me, so once again I just figured, "Fuck you and fuck everyone else around here. I will figure this shit out myself." It may have taken me a bit longer, but I did! I have done very well by learning to figure things out for myself, but as I have gotten older, I've realized that mindset isn't ideal and that in order for me to grow and evolve further, asking questions to the right people was going to be critical for me.

If you have questions and aren't met with a favorable response, find better people to ask. There are always good people out there who are willing to help out and share their experience with others. Another tool we have available today for getting answers to our problems is the Internet. We can literally learn about anything we want these days, we just have to know where to look and who to trust. That part won't always be easy, but once you do figure it out, all you have to do is ask the right questions. It won't always be free. I have seen people complaining about a seminar on flipping houses that was $200 per head, saying that they shouldn't have to spend money on something like that. Ok, great, no problem, see you later, because if that is your big concern, you most likely don't have the attitude to figure it out on your own anyway. I find things like this where there are people teaching about topics we want to know about extremely valuable. I am sure there are plenty of horrible seminars out there, but if you research it and know the person or team doing the seminar is legit, then taking the course will help your cause! I can't wait to go to my first Tony Robbins seminar now that I have more free time, and I will gladly pay to have an opportunity to hear his thoughts and be a part of his mindset for a short period of time. It will be fun and help me for the rest of my life. You often see ex-wrestlers giving wrestling seminars where you can pay to go and learn and ask questions from someone who has made it in the profession. Getting to hear the thoughts and advice from people like that for a wrestler could be the difference between making it big time or not at all! You are paying to ask the right person the questions you may have. This goes for all professions or activities.

Now, not everyone is going to be so kind as to offer their advice, as I have encountered quite a lot of people who don't really want to help out. I will never forget in WWE John Cena being very standoffish when out of curiosity I asked him one question. Usually, I wouldn't ask him anything wrestling related, but he did one thing very well, I noticed, that I was hurting myself on. The task at hand was getting thrown into the steel stairs near the ring. When hit correctly, it is effortless, as the top half of the stairs come unhinged and it looks a lot worse than it is. I was having to hit these stairs night in and night out for several weeks and, more often than not, they were not coming unhinged. My shoulder and hand were starting to pay the price. I simply asked one day, "Hey, John, how do you take those stairs so good?" He just said, "You will figure it out" as he walked away. You would think someone who has been lucky enough to have other people make him look so good and who supposedly cares about the business so much wouldn't mind helping someone out, but that wasn't the case. We are all going to encounter people like this. I simply asked around a bit more and realized that it was an easy fix and got the solution to my problem anyway. No hard feelings. I understand why he felt the need not to help and am totally ok with that. If you are met with deaf ears, it is ok, just move on to someone else. The quicker you can become comfortable asking questions and not worrying about looking stupid, the quicker you will figure things out. It is just a mindset of wanting to learn, so ask more questions and stop depriving yourself of more knowledge!

WE LEARN BY EXPERIENCING

To get the skills we need, there is no better way than getting your hands dirty, so to speak. While I am a big believer in the human mind being able to envision things, there is nothing like experiencing something for real. Growing up, the things I excelled at the most were the things I did and experienced the most. I was great at baseball, football, soccer, basketball, reading, and video games because so much of my time was spent on those activities. Eating is another thing I have gotten really good at, and why? Because all I do is eat! Life is too short to sit back and not experience. I can sit and do burpee conditioning drills in my head all day and night and while it may help me with my form mentally, it isn't going to get me in peak condition like doing the actual burpees will. That is one of the things I wish *The Secret* had gone into more depth about—the actual work and experiencing part of life that goes hand in hand with a positive mindset. It is imperative to have a positive mindset and to envision and believe, and I totally am of the belief that, when done properly, it helps attract people and situations into your life that align with your thoughts. But no matter how you slice and dice it, that cannot make up for actual experience and hard work. Take for example the year I sat back and watched jiujitsu DVDs and training videos. Sure, those helped to familiarize me with the different moves and techniques, but it was when I actually started training in jiujitsu that I began truly learning and understanding it.

There are millions and millions of wrestling fans and a certain portion are overly critical and judgmental and think wrestling is actually really easy. Well, one day, I saw one of these fans get the opportunity to get in the ring. He was severely overweight and did not appear to have any formal athletic training. He took one back bump, as we call it in wrestling, onto his back, which knocked the wind out of him. He flipped and flopped around before running to the bathroom crying. So let me just reiterate that there is nothing in this world that can make up for experience. And I am sure that is one experience that guy will never ever forget.

Anyone I have ever seen have a problem with the book *The Secret* always go off about the work part of it. I always have doubts these sorts of people even read the book. I just naturally understood that when our minds want something badly enough and we line up our thoughts accordingly, then our actual experiences and the work part will just happen effortlessly. For me that has always been the case, but people will be people.

We can look at all the pictures and videos of going hiking in a beautiful mountainous landscape and truly enjoy the pictures, but there is nothing like experiencing it for real, from the smells to the sounds to the actual sights. What I want you to get from this is that you shouldn't be afraid to go live life and make up all your own experiences. If there is stuff you want to get out and do in this lifetime, then figure out a way to get it done. If you want to get better at something, just keep doing it over and over and over. Life is meant to be experienced!

MUSIC MOTIVATES OUR SOUL

Who doesn't love music? It is something I enjoy every single day to create different emotions, to calm my mind, or to energize my body and spirit. Simply adding a particular type of music to a video could determine if you cry or if you are happy. It is used in almost every form of entertainment today from MLB players walking up to the plate for their at bat, pro fighters' and wrestlers' entrances, bodybuilders' posing routines, clubs, bars, movies, and anything else you can think of.

Ever since I was a kid, I have loved listening to music. I remember loving wrestling music and the emotions it created. To me one of the best parts of pro wrestling has always been the theme music and amped up theatrics that allow us to suspend our disbelief and live in the moment of our adrenaline and chaos. Anyone who remembers being a kid and hearing Hulk Hogan's "Real American" or Macho Man Randy Savage's "Pomp and Circumstance" (I just downloaded that right now and am listening as I write this, having flashbacks to my childhood) knows what I mean. Then you have someone like the legendary Stone Cold Steve Austin. When that glass shattered with his theme music, your felt that rush and knew someone was going to get their ass kicked. I still remember a time in 2012 when my music hit and the crowd roared so loudly the cameras shook. There is no greater feeling in the world than feeding on the energy and adrenaline of others!

Movies use music to help elicit certain emotions at key points and it never gets old. I love certain movies just because there is a particular song that makes me feel so good that it makes the overall movie even better for me. One that comes to mind is the classic comedy *Shallow Hal*. There is a dance floor scene where Hal (Jack Black) is on the dance floor dancing with the "hippo, giraffe, and the hyena" and this song called "Too Young" by Phoenix plays in the background. I could listen to that song over and over, as it just puts me in a good mood. In the *Terminator* movies, when they play the climactic music or the *Terminator* theme song, it creates such a strong emotion that I will forever be a fan.

Another way music has added to my life is through meditation. There are hundreds of meditation programs available that can help us to relax and focus our minds on love, health, money, and an array of other choices. There are mellowing relaxation mediations to help us fall asleep and sleep better (Holosync Dream Suite is my personal favorite).

Classical music is also a favorite of mine and I find it to not only be relaxing, but to get my mind working and it always seems to help me find my creative flow. I love to write while listening to classical music or just have it playing over the speakers in my house at times to create a chill and relax vibe.

I have always been more drawn to the sound and beat of a song than I am to the words. I have never been good at learning words to songs, and I am ok with that. The emotion the music creates for me is what I am after. As a kid, I always liked the instrumental versions better than the actual song with words, as it was just superior that way to me. I am also horrible at remembering the names of the musicians of a lot of the songs I listen to. There are people who love knowing everything about a particular musician and love studying the history of music and that is awesome. I just enjoy music for the emotion and that is pretty much where it begins and ends for me.

Our emotions are ours and ours alone and it is up to us to create the best emotions possible for ourselves. Music helps me do this. Next time you are feeling down and out or having a not-so-good day, maybe all it will take is hearing that one certain song to brighten your day!

TELEVISION TIMEOUTS

TV is a major part of life for most people. We are exposed to it at a young age and, in certain instances, it can be a great learning tool for kids. It is always there for us and it can provide endless hours of entertainment. It keeps us informed about local and worldwide news and even though there is a lot of negativity, a lot of valuable information is passed on as well. It can help take our minds off of some of life's problems and is there for us week in and week out with the programs we can't seem to live without. Not only are they in our homes, but they are now pretty much everywhere we go—gyms, restaurants, airports, airplanes, cars, and anywhere else you could possibly think of. They are a staple for many family gatherings and a great way to spend time having fun hanging out with friends. TVs can be a positive part of our lives, so by no means is this chapter meant to discourage the use of TVs altogether.

I do think that we should take breaks from watching too much TV—television timeouts—to give ourselves opportunities to do things we maybe wouldn't do. I look back at my life and there is a clear pattern for me where I'm not as productive when I spend large amounts of time in front of the TV. I particularly remember being in college after my baseball-playing days had come to an abrupt end. I was in school full time for Fitness Management, but was just lost. I knew I should probably finish school and get my degree, but I also wanted to wrestle. I had my work ethic, but I didn't have a direction yet to point it in. I would get home after school and just sit around and watch TV until I fell asleep.

I started viewing TV totally differently after spending time with former WWE World Heavyweight Champion Daniel Bryan. Dan loves learning and that is something I have always been obsessed with. His views on life always fascinated me, and I always appreciated him telling me about the books he had read. Dan mentioned that he didn't have cable or even a TV in his house (at least in 2012) and that always intrigued me. He just seemed to have a zest for life and what one would call an old soul. He always seemed happy and never spoke badly about people that I heard. He preferred experiencing things rather than sitting around watching TV. Now while having no TV or cable may be a bit extreme for most people, even me, it put the idea into my head about having TV timeouts where I would cut back on my TV consumption. I started doing this when I was on the road. I wouldn't turn the TV on in the hotel room unless I wanted a little life in the room while I was showering and getting ready. Instead, I would listen to audio books, read, or watch a match or two in the time I would have been watching TV, all things that drastically helped me in life. If there was a particular sporting event on TV that I wanted to see, I would catch part of the game or the ending, but most of the time, I didn't turn on the TV.

When home off the road, I had a habit of sitting down in front of the TV for 30 to 60 minutes upon waking up. It seemed so harmless but it ate up valuable time that I could have spent on better things. Now when I wake up, I come downstairs, put my headphones on, and listen to whatever audio book I am currently on. I cook my breakfast during this period and sit down and just focus on the task at hand. No matter how busy I get, I have already knocked out a good 20–40 minutes of listening to a book, which over the course of a year amounts to a lot! If I don't listen to an audiobook, I catch a wrestling match on YouTube or study my stocks for the day, all things that greatly help me in my life and make me happy. Just doing the hotel habit and the waking-up habit at home has added to my life greatly. I have not stopped watching TV altogether, but I have cut it down. It is just too easy to spend hours in front of the TV. If there is a particular show I want to see, like *Impractical Jokers*, I will allow myself 30 minutes to chill out and just relax. What I do may be too extreme for some, but take from it what you will and apply the TV timeout principle in your own way.

I will say though that saving television for periods when it could really help pass some time like after having surgery or for a situation where you need to take your mind off of something can be of great value. I like to splurge on some TV series when having some downtime. For example, after my recent ear and nose surgery where I had about a month of taking it easy and had to just sit back and relax to let the healing process work its magic, I enjoyed a few Netflix programs. I took this time to watch in entirety *It's Always Sunny in Philadelphia*, *Louie*, and *House of Cards*, three shows I had heard for years were incredible. I used that time to watch them while also still using that time to write, read, and listen to audio books.

According to an article in the *NY Daily News*, the average adult watches five hours of television a day! Can you imagine how much stuff you could get done with an extra five hours in your day? You don't have to cut it out entirely, but say you cut your viewing down to two or three hours a day. That extra two or three hours could amount to some great changes for you and your family if you fill that time with positive things. For those of you who have never worked out and really want to start, just imagine taking that extra couple of hours and beginning your lifelong journey to a happier healthier life. You can choose to do with that free time anything you want. If watching five hours of TV a day makes you happy and there is nothing else in your life you feel needs to be changed, then keep doing it and being happy. But if there are things you want to do to better yourself or to help others, then start taking action.

Like everything else in this book that I speak about, awareness is the key. There are so many amazing things to experience in life and while TV is a tremendous luxury and great tool to have at our disposal, let's not forget about the other great parts of life. We always have a choice in how we spend our time, so if you are feeling overwhelmed and feel like you could use more time in your day, take a look at your television consumption and see if reducing it can help solve the problem!

Section 4

RELATIONSHIPS

BREAKING UP

Breaking up with someone you are in an intimate relationship with absolutely sucks! There are no ifs, ands, or buts about it. I have been in several serious relationships, though for the most part I've chosen to remain single, especially during my younger years with the heavy wrestling schedule. Being in a relationship is a very serious matter, as is anything when love and feelings are at stake. From the different books I have read and my experiences with women, I feel we can educate ourselves about who we are as individuals so that we can do a better job of picking partners, enhancing our chances of staying together or at the very least ending the relationship on good terms. Not all relationships are meant to be forever. Some could last a month, others a year, and some much longer. The end game isn't always marriage and old age. I feel having a positive mindset and looking for the positives will help from the start if a breakup occurs. When you first start dating someone, ask them if they are friends with any of their exes. If they have an attitude about it and say no way, then you can pretty much see your fate if things end with you guys. I learned this the hard way, and I will never date someone if they cannot be friends. That is a negative mindset and I feel if kids or pets are involved, it spells disaster.

Another important thing when first meeting someone is communicating and seeing if you have similar views on sex and life in general. If she is someone looking to settle down and have kids and you are just looking to have some fun, you are setting yourself up for disaster. Great communication with your partner is something that needs to be there from the start. If there are problems from the start of a relationship, they are most likely only going to be worse the longer things go on.

If you take a chance on love, you are almost guaranteed to experience a breakup at least once, but by being prepared and educated, you increase your chances of dealing with that successfully. We have to love ourselves first and foremost and be happy with ourselves and what we are doing in our lives before adding someone to the mix. Being with someone to motivate you or make you better does not work. We must be mature and responsible humans to date, but so many of us aren't and that is why you see so many bad breakups and messy divorces. I firmly believe we should always be able to be friends after a breakup and be thankful for every moment of our time together and use that to help us move forward in life. A lot of people don't think that way, but I assure you it would make things so much easier for both parties if we all had that mentality.

Either way you have to give things time to calm down and find ways to keep yourself busy and involved. Oftentimes, when a breakup occurs, the couple continues to reach out to each other either through calling or endless texts. The best thing you could do is cut off all communication for a while and respect each other's decisions. If a woman breaks up with a man and that guy continues to call and pressure her, you are only lengthening the time before she comes around in a positive way and wants to talk to you. Obviously, this is easier said than done. But sitting around moaning or turning to excessive alcohol or drugs will only make matters much worse. We must deal with our feelings and emotions and choose to think positive thoughts of love and happiness towards that other person and just let time work its magic. Stay busy with work, get involved with local charities or homeless shelter activities, start a workout regimen, read, talk to family and friends, and just love yourself, and I promise you time will make things better eventually. Breaking up will always exist so if we can learn about it, understand it, and learn how to accept it responsibly, we can hopefully help diffuse or minimize any bad endings .

LOVE YOUR ANIMALS

Ever since I was a child, I have loved animals, dogs in particular. I have a great love and admiration for all animals, though, and truly wish every single animal could live a happy, love-filled existence. Unfortunately, animal cruelty is a very serious problem in our world and it breaks my heart when I hear about situations where beautiful, loving animals are mishandled and abused. I try to do a little every month by donating to the ASPCA , and I highly recommend everyone look into it. We have all seen the infomercials on TV and they are absolutely gut wrenching to watch. One of my huge life goals is to create a large animal facility in Las Vegas where dogs can be loved and cared for and have a safe, comfortable place to live if never adopted. Obviously, this type of facility will take a tremendous amount of money to create and maintain, but I can envision it and that means there is a way to get it done!

My first dog was a female black lab named Pebbles and I loved her so much. I will never forget the day we adopted her. When we got her to our house, she ran around our front yard so happy. I still drive by that old house in Las Vegas and remember all the happy memories I had there. One day after we got Pebbles, there was a dog wandering the neighborhood who looked similar to Pebbles. One of our neighbors put him in our fenced front yard thinking it was Pebbles. Nobody claimed him so we kept him and named him Bam Bam. Those two dogs provided so many great memories for our family. My sister and I used to take turns letting them sleep with us in our rooms and, to this day, I still have my pets sleep with me. I have always had a bond with dogs that I can't explain; I just love them beyond words.

When I was a senior in high school, I left the house one morning to drive to school and there was a beautiful female brindle pit bull puppy cuddled up in a ball on our doorstep. To this day, I don't know how she got there, but I am forever thankful for it. I had to hurry to get to school so I put a blanket in a big round hamper I had with some food and water and left her in my room. I ran home after classes and before football practice, and she had gone to the bathroom all over the basket and had food and water everywhere! I brought her outside and cleaned her up, and she ran and hopped around in excitement. My sister Carly and I convinced our mother to let us keep her and we named her Roxy. Roxy would wind up being an amazing dog that was always there for me when I needed her most. I remember after my baseball playing days came to an end in college being quite depressed for a good period as I tried to figure out how I could become a professional wrestler. While my friends were out partying and having fun, I would work out and stay home and read, knowing it would pay off someday. Roxy was there by my side for it all and to this day was still the most loyal dog I have ever had. She was so smart too. If I was watching too much TV and not paying attention to her, she would grab the remote and run it outside.

Putting my dogs down has always been extremely hard for me. While I do believe death is a great experience once we finally move on, it doesn't make it easier for those of us still here. Pebbles and Bam Bam were both old when Pebbles started experiencing some bad health problems. They had been together for twelve years, and we felt it would only be right to put them down together. I was a freshman in college and didn't go back when they put them down. To this day, I wish I could have held and kissed them in their final moments before moving on. I learned my lesson and will never let an animal of mine go without doing my best to be there for them.

Today, I have four dogs in my life—Shera, who is twelve, along with Secret and Sophie, a female French bulldog who keeps me very busy. I also frequently watch Sonny, my ex-girlfriend's male French bulldog. Shera recently was diagnosed with a mast cell tumor on her leg, and as anyone who follows me on social media saw, the photos weren't easy to look at. They removed the tumor, and she had a huge wound that was stapled shut. She was in tremendous pain. After further evaluations, it was brought to our attention that Shera had multiple cancer tumors, and her liver was also enlarged from cancer. We decided to go with the chemo pills therapy for her, as that has a very good success rate in most dogs. After several months of this treatment, her mast tumors have shrunk and her liver values have improved! We are hoping she can have another year or two of solid good health, but I have noticed she has slowed down a lot. She is always happy and in great spirits, but it is hard to watch an animal you love age before your very eyes. I try to go over and see my dogs at my dad's and bring Sophie over for playtime sometimes with Sonny, and it makes me happy to see all the dogs get along so well. They bring me so much happiness and being home more days than I'm gone now makes me appreciate them even more.

Having an animal comes with great responsibility. They rely on us to feed them and give them water and to make sure they are always taken care of. They depend on us to take them to the vet for checkups and for going on walks and playing. Yet so many loving animals go without a lot of these things because people who shouldn't have animals do. If you have a pet and you know you aren't there for it enough or can't give it the attention it should have, there is nothing wrong with looking for a loving home to take them. And if you see a dog that's gotten loose and is wandering in traffic, don't just blow past the animal with no concern! Pull over and get the dog to safety. It takes very little effort to call the animal shelter or the number on the tag so that the pet can be returned to its owner. It is the right thing to do. I still remember when I was in high school and my buddies and I went out for pizza one weekend. A dog had been hit on a busy road and was lying in the middle of the road bleeding. He couldn't move, but was still alive. I was filled with sadness and rage as I watched cars fly by at 50 mph, swerving around the dog or going right over it, just missing hitting it with their tires. I jumped out of the car and blocked traffic, and my friends and I got the dog to the sidewalk. We waited until an animal rescue could come, but sadly, it was too late and the dog passed away. Just don't be a piece of shit in life. It isn't that hard. Find an animal charity you like and please contribute what you can per month, and let's love the animals we have been blessed with on this planet. The love we give them is returned tenfold and will provide years of great memories.

FAMILY

Family is such an important part of life, yet for many of us, it causes a lot of pain and suffering. It seems for every happy family there are 20 dysfunctional ones. All families have their problems, but I'm talking about truly unhappy dysfunctional families here. Not all of us are raised by our biological parents, and when I use the word family, I mean the people we love and are closest with, whether biological or not.

There are so many different things we can talk about when it comes to family, and we all have our own unique situations. I love my family very very much, but I am not very close with them. I see them daily, as I had my house built five minutes from my father, and I moved my mother into an apartment suite attached to my house nearly a year ago. My sister lives in Reno and is happily married, and I will see her two or three times a year, usually during holidays. I wish she would move closer to her family, but respect her wish to live away.

I had a great childhood and my parents did a wonderful job raising my sister and me. My father worked as a bartender all his life, and my mother stayed at home for several years before returning to work. We had a hot dinner every night and always had plenty of food and drinks around the house to keep us happy and healthy. I have fond memories of my childhood and am very thankful to have come from a fairly "normal" family where nothing was ever too crazy and we celebrated the usual holidays. We always got to dress up and go trick-or-treating for Halloween and pig out and pass out with a belly full of amazing food every Thanksgiving (my favorite!). Our Christmases were phenomenal and my parents always made sure we got some of the stuff we wanted, even though I always wanted more more more! Easter was also a lot of fun, as my parents would hide eggs that my sister and I had colored earlier in the week. To me, the great thing about holidays isn't whether you believe what's behind them. It is spending time with your family and loved ones that make these holidays meaningful.

There is no situation that makes one family better than another. If a kid is raised by two women or two men, just because that isn't the norm doesn't make it wrong. Families come in all shapes and sizes and, as long as there is love and happiness inside, how they look to society on the outside is irrelevant. Coming from a family with a mother, father, and sister was great for me. I got along with my sister fairly well growing up, although as we got in high school we fought quite a bit. Looking back, I feel bad we ever fought, as I have always loved her very much, even though we aren't super close. We had many great times growing up together and would often do thing like play with our dogs Pebbles and Bam Bam in the dark in the garage, wearing heavy sweatpants and shirts for protection so the dogs could get us and lick and play with us. Another great memory I have is of my father taking me out for batting and fielding practice. The fact that he worked nights but still made time to do stuff like that to help me improve says a lot about him as a parent. My mother used to make me happy by baking these awesome homemade cookies and Rice Krispies Treats. I loved just being a kid and not having a worry in the world. Even though I had a good childhood and still live close to my parents, I have not always communicated well with them. I have tried very hard to get better at that. They are good human beings and, even though we are very different, they are my parents, so I have tried to improve in areas that I am not particularly good at. Being off the road now will allow me to be around more and give me the opportunity to enhance the lives of my family even more. While I may not have a perfect relationship with my family, it is pretty damn good. Many people out there did not have it as good as me or have suffered tragic situations with their families, so I am very thankful to have my family in my life.

The family we are born with, though, may not always be the right family for us. There are a lot of very bad people out there and they always seem to reproduce way more than the good people. I have known many people who had to cut off all contact with their loved ones because they were destructive alcoholics or drug addicts who stole from their loved ones to continue their high. In situations like this, or worse, it is imperative to get away from the situation if they are not willing to get help. Unfortunately, these sorts of things are common, and I truly feel for people who have to deal with this sort of thing. The only thing we can do in situations like this is love ourselves enough to do what is best for us and then do things differently when starting our own families.

Even those of us with happy families need to make an effort to maintain those relationships. I am trying to make more time to do family stuff and being home is an opportunity for me to make that happen. I would like to take my father to a Dodger's game and a football game in San Diego this year and do something nice with my mother and sister sometime as well. I was away from home for seven years for wrestling and absolutely hated the fact that I lived so far away. It just didn't feel right. I spoke with them often, but it just wasn't the same. I am beyond thankful to have them close now and to have my sister a short flight or a seven-hour drive away, which isn't all that bad. It seems families are growing apart more and more these days, and that shouldn't be the case. I have friends that have family get-togethers to bring everyone around, and I think that is just great. Even if you aren't super close with your family, attempting to bring everyone together and just trying to be happy is never a bad thing. We all have the power inside of us to change something for the better. It takes just one thought, one moment, one decision. Keeping a close family is worth that one moment.

Section 5

MONEY

MONEY

I am a firm believer that we are all meant to have the life we believe we should have. It isn't always clear and simple, but it starts with the mindset. A lot of us develop a negative mindset towards money stemming from childhood or instances in our lives where there was never enough. We must develop a positive mindset towards money and believe that there is an abundance of it in the world for everyone. Easier said than done, perhaps, but necessary. Wealth is a mindset. Not just with money, but with all things in life. A lot of us believe money can only be earned through employment and what other people choose to pay us. I am here to tell you that's wrong. Money can come from anywhere and anyone, but it takes truly opening your mind and releasing all negative thoughts towards it.

I love money because when you have enough money to live carefree, you can find your true self. When you have access to anything in life, your choices are not influenced by not having enough. I take great pride in knowing that I haven't given into certain things like drugs or pricier addictions, because I know who and what I am. It doesn't always turn out this way, though. You often see people get rich quick and it totally ruins their lives because they all of a sudden have access to a whole new realm of possibilities, but they don't truly know themselves. I'm not saying you can't be happy without money, or that you can't achieve love and knowledge without it. But not having to worry about money helps us see where we are in our lives.

There is a great quote from Benjamin Franklin I always try to remember: "Money never made a man happy yet, nor will it. The more a man has, the more he wants. Instead of filling a vacuum, it makes one." Remembering this has encouraged me to always strive for more knowledge and wisdom. But not having to worry about medical bills or emergencies or any other of life's problems and being able to say yes to anything you feel is good for you is freedom. I have had experiences in life where having more money would have resulted in a more positive outcome. So much good can be created with money and this is why the mindset of loving money is important.

Growing up I knew very little about money outside of the fact that it allowed me to get stuff I liked. The more of it I had, the more stuff I could get. I have great parents and they did an amazing job raising my sister and me, but they didn't teach us about money. I think it is safe to say the majority of kids aren't taught about money. It isn't until college that people start getting any idea about it. We cannot depend on the school system or anyone but ourselves to educate us and our loved ones. Whether you love money or hate it, we all need it in order to survive so it is imperative that we learn about it. I certainly do not agree with the phrase "money is the root of all evil." I believe that money gives people more options and we have a choice on how we use it. A lot of it comes down to our beliefs and who we are as human beings. I have always loved money, but my pride and my self-respect have led me to give everything I do my best effort and this has allowed me to grow hungrier for life as I have accumulated more money.

There are so many different things to learn about—checking accounts, savings accounts, debit cards, credit cards, stocks, bonds, CDs (certificates of deposit), treasury bills, real estate, and the list goes on and on. It can be very overwhelming, so many people avoid learning about the different ways we can have our money work for us. I am constantly reading books on money. Three books that have really helped me are *Rich Dad Poor Dad* by Robert Kiyosaki, *Money: Master the Game* by Tony Robbins, and *Total Money Makeover* by Dave Ramsey. I highly recommend everyone pick up these books and any other books on the topic you can get your hands on. *The Rich Dad Radio Show* is available on iTunes also, and even just listening to an episode here and there will greatly increase your financial intelligence. A big issue to overcome when it comes to money is fear. I was always terrified of the stock market or putting my money into retirement because I was unsure. After years of reading and learning, I was able to set aside those fears and let my money work as hard as I was. We all come from different backgrounds and have different levels of income, but we can all set goals with money and have a structured system and game plan. We don't all have to want to be millionaires or billionaires, but we should all want to be happy and enjoy life. Stressing about money has never made anyone happy. The ball is in our court, and we have to be aggressive about learning all that we can about money because it is what allows us to survive in today's world.

PINCHING PENNIES

For so many of us, money is tight. I have been there, and it isn't a good feeling. We have talked about a positive money mindset, but what are some ways to cut down and save some money along the way? What if I told you that you could potentially save yourself thousands of dollars a year simply by making some adjustments to your current routine? Well, you can, and it just involves applying a little thought and effort into some basic everyday things we take for granted. For example, how many people enjoy stopping on their way to work for a morning coffee at their favorite coffeehouse? Depending on where you go, that can cost from $2 to $6 depending on the type of drink you like to get. For the sake of simplicity, let's just assume a standard large coffee. Let's say on average it is $3 and you get one cup a day five days a week on your way to work. That comes out to $15 a week, $60 a month, and $720 dollars a year. All that just in one coffee a day. And some people do two, which is $1440 a year. If you simply used a thermo mug and brewed your own coffee every morning, that would cost around $100 per year, a big savings.

If you don't watch a lot of TV, cancelling your cable bill can save you a lot of money per year also. Some cable rates can go as high as $100 per month! If you are paying $70 per month for cable, cancelling can save you $840 dollars a year. If you just subscribe to Netflix, that costs $120 a year on average, saving you $720 dollars. Eating out all the time is another thing that costs a lot of money, especially when you eat the amount of food I do. When I was on the road, I was eating out multiple times a day. Now that I am home more and making most of my meals at home, I have saved so much money. I still go out to eat as a treat here and there, but nowhere near as frequently as I used to. Cooking your own food and storing it in plastic containers to take to work is a great way to pinch pennies.

If you love buying books and listening to audio books like I do, borrowing them from the local library is an option. I average two to three books a week and that adds up fast over the course of the year. I look at these as investments in myself and my future, so it is an expense I am ok with, but if you are a bit tight in the cash department, the local library could be your best bet! Bottled water is another big expense and the cost is highly marked up, especially at places like the movie theater or a sporting event. Investing in an Oko level-two filtration water bottle (a water bottle that will filter out all the impurities of tap water), which goes for around $25, can save you a lot of money, as well as the time it takes to stop for water. I carry one with me everywhere; it's a must for living on the road. For water at home, invest in a water filter, which can provide the same quality as bottled water.

Around the house, using toilet banks in the toilet bowls and not leaving the water running while brushing your teeth or washing your hands can help to save water and cut down on the monthly water bill. Adjusting the thermostat up or down just a couple degrees can also help pinch pennies, especially in the summer and really cold parts of winter. Simply wearing warmer clothes while inside during winter is an easy alternative to cranking the heater up.

There are plenty of other ways to pinch pennies, depending on your circumstances. Life is meant to be lived and experienced, and I in no way want you to deprive yourself of all the great things in life. Maybe you could buy one or two cups of coffee a week at the coffee shop and bring the rest from home, or cut down on eating out to once a week. If you are tight on cash, there are many things that you could possibly do without for a bit.

Some final ideas on saving money. Get a big five-gallon jug and put any coins you have accumulated into it at the end of the day. By the end of the year, you'll have a significant amount of money. If you enjoy traveling and use credit cards in a responsible way, paying them off every month, then frequent flier airline credit cards are a must have! Typically, you get a mile per dollar spent, and if you use these credit cards enough, you will rack up some serious frequent flier miles! This can save you hundreds of dollars, if not thousands in flights. You usually get a free bag checked with the cards, saving you that nasty $35 baggage fee. Also, if you use them a lot, it can help get you bumped up to first class sometimes, and that makes flying a little more enjoyable. There is always a way to pinch pennies—we just have to be creative!

EMERGENCY FUND

I first learned of the importance of having an emergency cash fund from reading Dave Ramsey's book *The Total Money Makeover*. An emergency fund is a reserve of money you have put away either in a checking account or a safe to cover any sudden costs like an automobile crash, hospital visit, or house maintenance issues. You should have enough to cover three to six months of expenses. The reason we should all have some sort of emergency fund is that we truly don't know what is going to happen. I am all about being positive and keeping my thoughts on track, but that doesn't mean we shouldn't be prepared just in case. Over 75 percent of people will have a major negative financial event happen to them in any ten-year period. It is only wise to err on the side of caution. How much is enough for an emergency fund? I say the more the better, but it depends on your current situation. A good starting point is to add up all your monthly bills and expenses to get a ballpark idea of what it costs for you and your family to survive each month. Multiply that by three, four, five, or six months to get your savings goal.

I know this can seem difficult if money is extremely tight. But if you save even $25 a week for this fund, that will add up to $1,300 a year. If there are weeks you can add more to the fund, do it. The point is to make an effort and be aware of the benefit of having this fund. It will give you and your family peace of mind knowing that if you suddenly lose your job or something hits you hard financially, you have some sort of reserve to fall back on temporarily. I personally remember a situation back when I wrestled in Tampa for FCW. I lived week to week like most wrestlers and was not financially educated one bit. All I knew was that I made enough money to survive doing what I loved, and I had food and my supplements, which were an investment for my job. I had little to no savings and most certainly didn't have an emergency fund. My car, a Nissan Altima (which my sister now proudly has), suddenly had four bad tires. Three had holes in them and the fourth was so worn out that it needed to be replaced also. I needed my car to drive to shows and practice, but I was paying off credit card debt at the time and had no options for how to pay for four new tires. Luckily, my best friend, Pat Buck, was able to bail me out and lend me the cash, but it was embarrassing to not be prepared for a situation like that. I paid Pat back as soon as I could and it taught me a very valuable lesson. I never want to be in that boat ever again.

Even if having three to six months' worth of expenses doesn't seem doable to you, please make an effort. Just set something aside every week and forget about it. Don't cave in and use it for anything, unless there is a true emergency. Having to go and get a pack of cigarettes or a bottle of booze doesn't classify as an emergency, either. Start small and work your way up and before you know it your emergency fund will be in place!

GOOD DEBT BAD DEBT

Debt results when one party borrows money from another party. Most of us in our lifetimes are going to experience debt of some sort. We have to incur debt for a lot of life's bigger purchases like houses and vehicles. Not all debt is created equal though. Good debt is debt that increases your net worth and can help generate value. Bad debt is debt that decreases our wealth and is used to buy goods or services that have no lasting value. Below is a sample list of good debt and bad debt.

GOOD DEBT

- Technical or college education
- Business ownership
- Investing
- Real estate

BAD DEBT

- Vehicles
- Clothes
- Credit cards
- Anything you can't afford

Living in Las Vegas, I see a lot of people who aren't wealthy take on an incredible amount of bad debt to appear so. It is a very common thing that isn't limited to Las Vegas.

The more I learn about money and wealth, the more fascinating it gets to me. Our entire world is structured around this one thing. Unfortunately, we don't learn about it in school and it is up to us to learn unless we come from a family that understands money and passes that knowledge down. If you want to learn about money, I recommend *Rich Dad Poor Dad* by Robert Kiyosaki. I think he gets it right when he talks about humans as being in a rat race, which Wikipedia defines as "an endless, self-defeating, or pointless pursuit. It conjures up the image of lab rats racing through a maze to get the 'cheese' much like society racing to get ahead financially."

Years ago, I used to go to lunch once a week with Stu Bennet, otherwise known to wrestling fans as Wade Barrett. I was going through my ankle injury at the time, and that was when I really started reading to better myself. Coincidently, Stu had also begun doing this, and we would sit around at a Hooters or a Ranch House Grill and bullshit and talk about any new books we had come across. We still shoot each other books to this day. Something we have always joked about is "just trying to get out of the ol' rat race." The world is designed the way it is and unless we educate ourselves on finances and make a true effort to escape, we may forever be chasing the cheese. I don't know about you, but I want to believe life is meant to be lived and for us to have everything we desire, so I want to do everything in my power to ensure that mindset. I have said it before and will say it here that we should all be reading or listening to at least one financial book a month. It takes time to absorb this stuff and repetition helps. Every one of us has a different situation though, and I'm not going to tell you getting a financial education is enough to make you rich. It takes a lot of things for that to happen, but we increase our chances of improving our security if we learn all we can.

I have always invested in myself and my body for professional wrestling. I knew the money and time spent improving myself would ultimately bring me wealth and security in that field. I always looked at the money I spent on nutrition and supplements as good debt and to this day, I still feel that way. But not all of my debt has been good. When I first got signed by WWE at 22 years old, I bought a truck that was too expensive for where I was at that point in my life. I needed a truck big enough to pack my stuff in so I could drive to Atlanta from Las Vegas to begin my pro wrestling career. I should have bought a truck that was less expensive or driven a U-Haul to Atlanta and bought something there. So many of us overspend on vehicles. I see people all the time here who are struggling but have a $600 car payment every month. Speaking from experience, you cannot get out of the rat race if you are just barely getting by every month. You have to be able to save something and invest if you are ever going to break free.

Credit cards are a great thing to have and most definitely have a place, but when we spend money we don't have, that creates a very dangerous situation. The average credit card debt per household is somewhere in the $15000 range and that isn't counting things like student loans, mortgages, and car loans. There are always going to be emergencies, and if we don't have an emergency fund in cash, then credit cards can be useful. But if you are someone who runs up credit debt and then refinances your house or takes out a loan to pay off your cards, just to run them up again, you have most likely lost control.

It seems like the middle class is getting smaller and smaller and we are becoming a world of rich and poor. It takes effort and hard work along with financial education to move up, and if you aren't willing to learn and grow then nothing will ever change. The world owes us nothing and it is nobody's job but our own to take control and learn all that we can to better ourselves and those around us. Our world teaches us to simply be employees and that working for others is the only way to make it and that just isn't true. Sure, it is one way to make money and support ourselves, but there are so many different ways to earn money. We must understand good debt and bad debt by increasing our financial knowledge and then figure out a game plan to escape this so-called rat race. Some people might be interested in stocks while real estate appeals more to others, and some will want to be involved in everything. We all have different situations, but nothing bad will come from increasing your knowledge about money. Make a list of your good and bad debt and see if there are any changes you can make to improve your current situation. Perhaps making a goal board with your financial goals would be a nice follow-up to get you on track. Make good decisions one day at a time and it will positively affect you for the rest of your life.

Section 6

PERSONAL RESPONSIBILITY

TEXTING WHILE DRIVING

Texting or using our cell phones when driving is something very new for us as a society. I am 100 percent guilty of doing this myself. I have made it a habit to try and limit how much I do this, even though much of my time is spent inside rental cars and on the road. Driving is a privilege and many of us abuse that privilege by doing things such as texting that distract us from giving 100 percent of our attention. Just recently, I was driving and watched a young woman make a left turn while she was on her phone and she didn't look up once. Her car was completely wrecked on the driver's side so maybe she was trying to balance the other side out! Point is, that it is beyond dangerous. She may have seen there were no cars coming somehow, but what if a kid was crossing the road? I also recently saw a man driving in heavy LA traffic while on his phone, and he did not see the cars stop in front of him and ran straight into the back of them at about 35 to 40 mph. Most of us have probably been guilty of using our phones while driving and while this book probably won't cause you to stop altogether, I can ask that we all try our best to resist the urge. Don't use your phone in high traffic areas or areas kids or animals could be in. I now try to talk on Bluetooth instead of texting someone. Many newer cars are capable of connecting to our cell phones so you can do this without a Bluetooth headset. I have bought dash cams for both my vehicles so I never have to hold my phone, or I do my best not to look at it unless I am pulled over. I will even use an app like Voxer, which is a walkie-talkie that allows you to talk back and forth without texting. Statistics show we are 23 times more likely to be involved in an accident while using our cell phones behind the wheel, so it just makes sense not to! Be smart and considerate of each other and think about more than just the immediate task at hand. I'm sure there are people reading this who have lost someone in an accident because of cell phones, and I cannot even imagine the pain and suffering that must cause. Let's all do our best to make the world as safe as we can. It takes just a split second of being distracted to change our lives—or someone else's—forever.

DRINKING AND DRIVING

Living in Las Vegas, where many places are open 24 hours and alcohol is on a never-ending tap, drinking and driving is something I became aware of quite early. We have all been lectured on drinking and driving, especially when we first learn to drive, but it seems no matter how many tragic stories we hear, it doesn't stop us from doing it. One story that did have an impact on me was when my first professional wrestling trainer, Bill Demott, lost his daughter Keri Anne to a drunk driver at the age of 20 years old. He had a blood alcohol level of .132 and hit her head on. To this day, it saddens me that he lost a daughter he loved so much. He is doing great things in trying to help raise awareness of the repercussions of drunk driving.

There is nothing wrong with wanting to drink and have a great time, but it is important to take proper measures to prevent drunk driving. This could be planning on only having a drink or two or having a designated driver. There are also cabs, and now Uber, which makes going out and drinking much less stressful. It is about adopting the mindset that if you are drinking, getting behind the wheel isn't an option. It is making it a habit each and every time, and never letting anyone you know make that mistake. If you are one of those people who feel the need to get behind the wheel after drinking, give your keys to a friend beforehand and make sure they understand they are not to give them back until you are sober. This cannot be stressed enough. Each time it gets through to one person, that could save someone's life. Drinking and driving is not acceptable or worth it, so let's just accept this as a truth and do our best to continue raising awareness.

CUTTING DOWN ON PLASTICS

Plastic has changed the way we live our lives and is everywhere we look, from the bottles we drink our water out of to the credit cards we use to buy our groceries, many which are packed in plastic and then bagged in more plastic. It has made our lives much easier and made goods less expensive but it is also going into our oceans and polluting our world at a rate that is unheard of. It is estimated that 1.6 billion pounds of plastic is dumped into the ocean each year! That is an alarming number and it is rising.

It doesn't look like it will get better anytime soon, but we can each try cutting back on the amount of plastics we use and make sure to always dispose of the plastics we use in a recycling bin. I drink a lot of water and when I am on the road, it can sometimes be hard to control how much bottled water I consume, as I don't like to drink tap water. A great solution to this is a filtered water bottle, like the OKO bottle I mentioned in the section about saving money. It is perfect when traveling in a car or stuck in a hotel room, as I can drink all the tap water I want without going through multiple plastic bottles. For when I am home, I have bought glass bottles that can be reused. I find cold water stored in the glass bottles tastes more refreshing than water kept in plastic. You can find all different types on Amazon if you are interested. I have a filtered water system for my home as well and keep one or two plastic bottles that I will reuse for the gym when I don't want to bring a glass bottle out with me. So rather than going through ten bottles of water a day, I use the same one, and over time that makes a difference.

Another thing I can control when home is using reusable grocery bags when I shop. You can keep the bags stored away or in your car trunk so that you don't always use disposable plastic bags. Little things like this make a difference and raise awareness because other people checking out will notice and hopefully change their behavior too. It is very simple—if we don't do anything, nothing will ever change, but if we attempt to make a difference, it at least helps to some degree. Obviously, the ultimate solution is finding a better way to dispose of our plastics than dumping them in the ocean, but until that time comes, we must try and make a difference. If you want more information about plastics and plastic trash, I recommend the book *Plastic* by Susan Freinkel and the documentary *Plastic Paradise* on Netflix. They are both eye-opening.

WATER CONSERVATION

Until we can find a way to tap into our vast oceans for water in a cost-effective way, we absolutely must be conscious of the way in which we use water. There are more humans on our planet than ever before and that number just keeps increasing. With more people comes more demand for water. They say the average human consumes between 80–100 gallons per day and, considering there are billions of people in our world, that number is astonishing! The human body itself is 50–67 percent water, so there is no doubt we need water to survive. It only makes sense that we examine how we have used water in the past and how we are using it now. There are many things we can do to save water and they aren't difficult. For example, bath faucets of yesteryear would use around 2 gallons per minute and bath faucets of today use around 1 gallon per minute. Something as simple as switching out your bath faucet could make a big difference over time. Same thing with shower heads, which, after toilets and baths, use the most water in most homes. Old shower heads typically use 5 gallons of water per minute, but new water-saving shower heads use only 2 gallons per minute.

I remember when I read Arnold Schwarzenegger's autobiography how impressed I was with the part on water conservation. Up to that point in my life, I really hadn't given it much thought, but his words really woke me up to how I use water. For example, I used to let the water run on full blast the entire time I was brushing my teeth. I wasn't doing this because I wanted to waste water. Truth be told, the water was always calming to me and it was just a habit I started as a kid. After realizing how wasteful that is, though, I began keeping the water off and only turning it on when I needed a bit of water. Same for when I shave my head, wash my hands, or wash my face. I always do my best now not to leave the water running. If you are a parent, teach your kids this so it becomes second nature. Showering is another way to overuse precious water. I love a good hot shower, but setting a time limit or at least not staying in there for however long we like will definitely help. I do my best to be in and out in ten minutes or less these days and am shooting for five minutes as a personal goal. Another cool way to save some water around the house or apartment is using these things called toilet banks. They are just water-filled bags that hang inside the toilet bowls out of sight. They allow the tank to fill up faster with less water so we don't flush extra water down the toilet. The performance of the toilet isn't sacrificed, and I have noticed a savings of over thirty dollars a month from using these things throughout my house. These are just a few things we can do to conserve water, as well as save money. Along with many of the other sections of this book, the idea is to just be conscious of it. When you remain conscious about your surroundings, small changes become second nature very quickly.

GOING SOLAR

Energy consumption was something I never really paid much attention to until quite recently. I just paid NV Energy my monthly bill and my energy needs were taken care of for the most part. Then one day I walked into a hardware store and they had a representative there from SolarCity, a company that provides solar power for homes. They explained to me how leasing solar panels through them, with the option to buy eventually, would save me a lot of money. Considering I live in Las Vegas where it isn't uncommon for the summer sun to scorch the desert at temperatures of 115 degrees, you can see how this may have piqued my interest. Every state has different rules when it comes to solar energy, but anything that can help our planet and save us some money in the process is a good thing in my book. Since making the switch to solar, I save on average $500 to $600 a year. I have a good-sized house and it consumes quite a bit of power with things like a pool, hot tub, cold tub, and two air conditioning units. The amount of power the house uses is pretty significant in the summer months. The solar panels produce enough energy to run my house during the day, and then I use Nevada Power for my nighttime power. It saves you money and you don't have to do anything outside of setting up the install. It costs nothing to have them come out and inspect the rooftop and design a model for your home or for them to do the installation. Once the process is finished and you begin using your solar power (which runs on its own), all you have to do is pay your monthly power bill. The following is a list of advantages and disadvantages of solar power to help give you a little more information on the subject. Every little bit helps though and I found the process to be very smooth and effortless. May the power be with you!

ADVANTAGES:

- Solar is renewable energy. Unlike other power sources, the sun's energy is unlimited and is a very consistent energy source that we can count on to be here every day.
- Solar energy is environmentally friendly.
- Solar panels are reliable.
- Solar cells make no noise while collecting energy.
- In the long run, solar electricity is cheaper than buying it from the power company.
- If you produce excess energy, you can sell it back to the power company.
- Solar technology is constantly improving.
- Solar energy creates zero pollution.

DISADVANTAGES:

- Solar power cannot be gathered during a storm, on a cloudy day, or at night.
- If buying solar panels, the cells and panels are quite expensive. Again, renting from someone like Solar City or a similar company eliminates those costs.
- For larger homes, current solar panels have trouble producing enough energy. Use of the power company typically is needed for nighttime use of power.

CLOSING THOUGHTS

Thank you for taking the time to read this book. My goal is to help inform and raise awareness in areas that I have had the opportunity to read and learn about, as well as experience. I truly love learning and increasing my own self-awareness and knowledge and being able to share that with my fans and people who are maybe meeting me for the first time. We should never stop learning or become complacent in life, no matter what our current situation is. Our minds are like our muscles—they need constant stimulation in order to truly grow and flourish. I realize that many people may think being a professional wrestler and writing a motivational book don't go hand in hand, but I refuse to just be one thing in life and have it end there. Everything I am and am known for in my life today is because of my mindset and many of the things I speak about in this collection of my thoughts. I guess if you get nothing else from this, I just want you to realize that the power of God lies inside each and every one of us. It is up to us to realize this power and decide what it is we want and then to go for it. Life is an amazing journey and it will have its ups and downs, but if we can keep an optimistic mindset and continue to grow, anything is possible. Thank you again for joining me on this journey and always remember—start full, end empty, say thank you, and feed me more!

THANK YOU

I want to say thank you one last time. This book is the beginning of a whole new chapter in my life, and I'm beyond grateful to have had the opportunity to share it with you, the reader. Writing most definitely isn't the easiest of tasks for me, as I typically enjoy more physical activities, but I can say I truly enjoyed every second I spent working on this. All I ask is that if you have some extra time and could leave a review on Amazon, it would be greatly appreciated. Until next time, stay positive, smile more, and stay hungry!

—Ryback Reeves

HUNGRY FOR MORE?

Visit <u>Feedmemore.com</u> and sign-up to receive action-packed motivational messages every week and I'll include exclusive email-only discounts on select <u>Feedmemore.com</u> items. You can shop for great merchandise on the site and order quality Feed Me More natural supplements.

Feed me more, you say? No problem! Join me weekly on my podcast, *Conversation with The Big Guy*, along with co-host Pat Buck. The podcast is available on iTunes and Stitcher. Until next time, my friends, stay hungry!

ABOUT THE AUTHOR

Ryback Reeves is best known for his wrestling persona, The Big Guy Ryback. Traveling the world screaming his war cry of Feed Me More, he captivated millions across the globe, allowing him to become one of wrestling's most recognizable characters. Although he is thankful for his time wrestling (he still performs most weekends), he wanted to have a bigger opportunity to help people outside the ring. Since leaving his full-time TV job behind, he has successfully launched his podcast *Conversation with The Big Guy*, <u>FeedMeMore.com</u>, his personal website for everything Ryback, and his natural supplement line Feed Me More Nutrition. Ryback spent countless hours traveling over the years and listening to book after book in search for more in life. You get an insight into some of that knowledge and the experience behind it here in *Wake Up, It's Feeding Time*. Thank you, thank you, thank you.

Printed in Great Britain
by Amazon